Welcome to
ancient
Greece

Text editing: Margaret McGlin
Cover - Layout: Efthimis Dimoulas

© 2016 "AGYRA" Publications, D.A. PAPADIMITRIOU SA
   This edition, March 2020
   271 Lampros Katsonis & G. Papandreou Str. – Agii Anargyri, P.C. 13562
   Tel.: 210 2693800-4 • Fax: 210 2693806-7
   Central: AGYRA-POLYCHOROS, 124 Solonos Str. - Athens, P.C. 10681
   Tel.: +30 210 3837667 • Fax: 210 3837066
   e-mail: info@e-agyra.gr • www.e-agyra.gr

ISBN: 978-960-547-228-3

Country of origin: Greece

MARIA KAZANTZIDIS

Welcome to ancient Greece

A journey to the classical era of Greece

Illustration: EVA KARANTINOU

Translated from Greek into English
Kiriaki Papakonstantinou
BA English Language & Literature / MA Psycholinguistics / DIPTRANS - DPSI
Chartered Linguist (Translator) / Translators - Interpreters Trainer
Member of the Chartered Institute of Linguists in London

Scientific consultant
Xanthi Proestaki
Dr of Archaeology and History of Art

AGYRA
publications

ANCIENT GREECE AT A GLANCE

Greece is a beautiful country with a long history covering tens of centuries.

If you have decided to visit Greece or if you're already there, it is important to know some things about the history and culture of this land. Its borders spread over three continents; for Ancient Greece was not just a country, but a culture without borders...

IN THE BEGINNING

Ancient authors considered the first populations that inhabited Greece – Cretans, Lelegs, Carians, and Pelasgians – ancestors of the Greeks.

During the second millennium BC, four major Greek tribes spread in Greece: the Dorians, the Achaeans, the Ionians, and the Aeolians. They mingled with the local populations, thus giving birth to three great civilizations: the Cycladic (about 3200 BC - 1100 BC), the Minoan (about 2000 BC – 1300), and the Mycenaean (about 1750 BC - 1060 BC). This era is called the Bronze Age, as weapons, tools, and armor are made of bronze.

The decline of the Mycenaean civilization, due to wars and natural disasters, was followed by the period of the Greek Dark Ages (about 1100 BC - 800 BC). It was called that because there are no written sources available for this period. It is also called Geometric, or the Iron Age, as iron replaces copper in making weapons and utensils.

The 7th and 6th century BC is a rather creative period up to 500 BC. This is the Archaic Era. Arts flourish and Greeks travel to other places, colonize them and thus Hellenism expands. Even Marseille is a Greek colony founded by the residents of Phocaea. Colonization renders the Greeks one of the greatest commercial and naval power of the era.

Greece is divided into independent city-states, either conflicting or uniting against common threats.

Then comes the Classical Period. It is the period from 500 to 336 BC, when culture and arts flourishes as never before. The city of Athens is powerful and dominates the other city-states under the leadership of Pericles. Sometime later (in the mid-4th century BC) Macedonia started rising as a power. With the powerful Macedonian army, King Philip II and Alexander the Great expanded Hellenism as far as India. Then, the great Hellenistic kingdoms of the Successors of Alexander the Great were founded, where Greek sculpture and literature flourished.

Eventually, the Romans conquered Greece and made great works of engineering, donations to cities, and temples – inspired by Greek culture. Ancient Greek history is so vast that one could talk about it for months. This book aims to provide the reader with the opportunity to mentally travel to Ancient Greece and discover the fundamentals of classical Greek culture. This period begins with victory of the Greeks over the powerful Persians. Having achieved such a great feat, the Greeks establish an unprecedented culture…

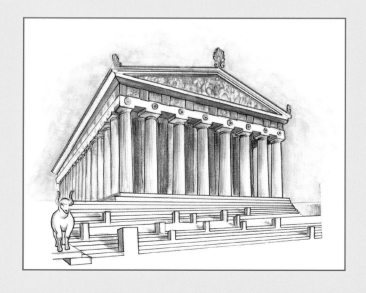

Abdera

Pella

Philippi

Dodona

Mount Olympus

A
E
G
E
A

Thermopylae

Delphi

Eretria

Thebes (Boeotia)

Marathon

Corinth

Eleusis

Athens

Nemea

Isthmia

Piraeus

Lavrion

Olympia

Salamis

Mycenae

Sounion

Argos

Epidaurus

I
O
N
I
A
N

Pylos

Sparta

S
E
A

CRETE

Knossos

6

Troy
Assos
Pergamon
Lesbos
Phocaea
Chios
Clazomenae
PENINSULA
OF MYCALE
Teos
Ephesus
Samos
Myus
Priene
Miletus
Halicarnassus
Kos
Rhodes

PERIODS OF THE ANCIENT GREEK HISTORY

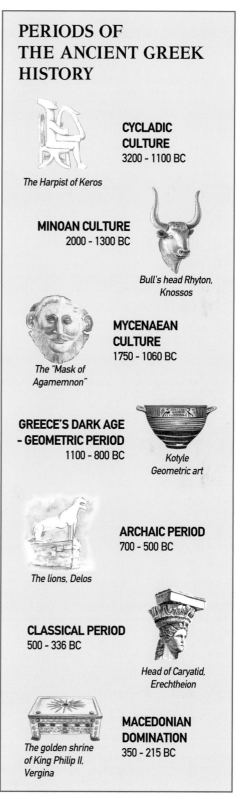

CYCLADIC CULTURE
3200 - 1100 BC

The Harpist of Keros

MINOAN CULTURE
2000 - 1300 BC

Bull's head Rhyton, Knossos

MYCENAEAN CULTURE
1750 - 1060 BC

The "Mask of Agamemnon"

GREECE'S DARK AGE - GEOMETRIC PERIOD
1100 - 800 BC

Kotyle Geometric art

ARCHAIC PERIOD
700 - 500 BC

The lions, Delos

CLASSICAL PERIOD
500 - 336 BC

Head of Caryatid, Erechtheion

MACEDONIAN DOMINATION
350 - 215 BC

The golden shrine of King Philip II, Vergina

PREPARING FOR THE JOURNEY

Greece is located south-east of Europe, on the southernmost tip of the Balkan Peninsula, in the Eastern Mediterranean. The Ancient Greek world extended from contemporary Italy to the northern coast of Africa, and from the coast of present-day Turkey and Syria to southern France! In the era of Alexander the Great, actually, the Greek world extended to China!

HOW TO GET TO GREECE

You can get there several ways... The easiest and fastest way is by plane, especially if you live in a distant country. You could also come by boat, enjoying the beautiful blue sea. Also, you can come by train or car so as to admire the landscape.

However, if you wished to visit Ancient Greece, only two choices would be available: either by boat or on foot.

If travelling on foot, you should have an animal, horse or donkey, to carry your luggage. The rich were able to travel more comfortably, as they had carriages and were escorted by slaves to protect them from the frequent raids by bandits. However, most people then preferred boat trips, although there was always the danger of pirates.

In any case, travelling at that time lasted several days or even months, depending on the distance one had to cover.

WHAT'S GREECE LIKE?

Greece is mainly a mountainous country with many rivers, several lakes, and about two thousand five hundred islands! Most of the country is surrounded by sea, thus beaches are countless. Mountains rise high and wild, while they are snowcapped almost all year round! They harbour many wild animals, bears, and wolves, while some beautiful forests grow there as well. Greece is a very fertile land, as there are many rivers running through the whole country emptying into the sea.

WHAT'S THE WEATHER LIKE?

Modern Greece has temperate climate, this means mild and wet, with rainy winters and very hot and dry summers. In ancient times, however, winters were colder and summers cooler than nowadays.

WHAT TO TAKE WITH ME

If you visit Greece in summer, make sure you bring along a pair of sandals, a hat, airy and light-colored clothes, a sunscreen to protect you from the sun and, of course, don't forget your swimsuit! Yet, if it is winter, make sure you bring along warm and waterproof clothing, an umbrella, and comfortable winter shoes.

WHERE TO STAY

You should keep in mind that Greece is a country with many visitors every year. It is also the country where hospitality was "born" along with respect for the foreigners and travelers... so, your stay will not be a problem.

There are small hostelries and cozy rooms to let where you can spend the night, as well as luxurious and comfortable modern hotels.

WHAT IF I GET HUNGRY?

There is nothing easier in Greece than enjoying a great meal! There are restaurants and taverns serving all kinds of food almost around every corner! Afterall, Greece is the homeland of the Mediterranean diet!

Even if you were a traveler in ancient times, you could have a meal at inns or small taverns, while you could find food in the marketplace as well. You could always have the opportunity to participate in a festival offering sacrifices to the gods. After the sacrifice, ancient Greeks would grill the meat of the sacrificed animals and offer it to the votaries and pilgrims. There, you could try food rather similar to contemporary Greek cuisine: a variety of fish, grilled meat or stew, several types of cheese, lots of fruits and vegetables, wine, and of course olive oil... The ancient Mediterranean Diet!

WHAT IF I GET SICK?

All over Greece, on each and every island or mountain, you can find infirmaries and daylong consulting rooms. For more severe cases, there are modern hospitals in every big city.

But what if you got sick in ancient Greece? That would be no problem at all! You are in the country where medicine was born! All you have to do is to go to one of the numerous shrines of Asclepius (see page 42) and follow the instructions of the priests, or alternatively resort to physicians who follow Hippocrate's therapeutic approach (see page 42)

THE GODS OF ANCIENT GREECE

Ancient Greeks believed in many gods; they were polytheists. As early as antiquity Greeks felt the need to understand and interpret the world around them – life, death; nature itself. Thus, everything surrounding them, either visible or invisible, was identified with and related to a god. So, Greeks fashioned their gods resembling them – with human flaws, passions and habits – as to be more easily identified with them. Traditionally, there were twelve ancient Greek gods and they lived on top of Mount Olympus, the highest mountain in Greece.

BUT, WHO WERE THESE GODS, ANYWAY?

Zeus is the leader and father of most gods, deities, and heroes. He is the god of balance and harmony in the universe, storm, wind and lightning. He is the protector of foreigners, vows, and state institutions, retributive of injustice, but also merciful to the weak. Yet, he is all but faultless, except his passion for beautiful women, either mortals or goddesses, thus becoming the father of numerous gods and heroes.

Hera is the queen of the gods, sister and lawful wife of Zeus. She is the raw model of the perfect wife, protector of marriage and the lady of heaven. She is also

very jealous – which makes perfect sense considering the innumerable romantic adventures of her husband, Zeus.

Poseidon is Zeus' brother, the god of the seas and all water. He is the protector of sailors, while at the same time he can raise storms and earthquakes with his trident. He can have islands emerge from the sea, calm waves down and create springs. His fault is his rage.

Athena is the favorite daughter of Zeus and Metis, daughter of Uranus and Tethys. She is the goddess of wisdom, patroness of arts, music, justice, and cities. She is also the goddess of works of peace and just war as well, inspiring courage to warriors, healing, and predicting the future. She taught people the cultivation of olive trees, sculpture, architecture, shoemaking, metallurgy; thus, she was adored and worshiped as few other gods were.

Demetra is the goddess of agriculture, protector of women and laws governing their lives, marriage, and society.

Aphrodite is the most beautiful of the Olympian goddesses, the goddess of love, fertility, and vegetation. She symbolizes blossoming and withering, life, and death. She is the lawful wife of god Hephaestus and mistress of god Ares – who is the father of her son, the god Eros.

Hephaestus is the son of Hera, born by the goddess alone for revenge on Zeus for his infidelities; he is lame and ugly by birth. He is the creator of fire, lightning, and volcanoes. He is the most skillful blacksmith, who made the chariot of the Sun, as well as Zeus' scepter and throne.

Apollo is the son of Zeus and mortal Leto, daughter of the titans Coeus and Phoebe – twin brother of goddess Artemis. He is the god of light, music, and the greatest

legislator. He can wreak death and disease, being at the same time a healer god. His most significant quality is clairvoyancy. He is the most handsome of all gods and the personi-fication of eternal youth.

Hermes is the son of Zeus and the nymph Maia. He is the messanger of gods and, apart from being very intelligent, he is also the cunningest of all gods as well. He is the protector of adolescents, flocks, roads, trade, and theft, scholars, health, sleep, and dreams. He is the god of fertility, as well as the one who escorts the dead on their journey to the Underworld.

Ares is the son of Zeus and Hera. He is the god of war, the most hated of all gods. He is always accompanied by his two sons, Deimos and Phobos, who represent terror and fear, respectively.

Hestia is Zeus' sister and the senior goddess of fire. She is the protector of home, family, and the city.

Artemis is the daughter of Zeus and mortal Leto, daughter of the titans Coeus and Phoebe – twin sister of Apollo. She is a virgin goddess, protector of wildlife and hunting, who can wreak death with her arrows.

judge of mortals, cruel and stony hearted; and, of course, he is particularly hated by people. His wife is Persephone, the daughter of goddess Demeter.

Dionysus is the son of Zeus and mortal Semele who lives on Earth. He is the patron god of viticulture and the one who taught mortals how to make wine and gave them the vine. He is the god of vegetation and protector of nature, art, entertainment, and fun. He lives in forests with his lunatic company of lesser deities, the satyrs and maenads.

Apart from the Twelve Olympians there were two more equally important gods: Hades, who lives in the Underworld and Dionysus who lives on Earth.

Hades is Zeus' brother and god of the Dead and the Underworld. He is the

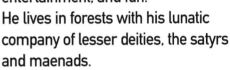

MYTHOLOGY AND HEROES

Mythology consists of all the stories and myths with which ancient Greeks tried to explain the creation of the world and trace their own origin. Mythology comprises stories about the relationships between gods who shaped human fate; between gods and humans, through which peoples, heroes and traditions are born; and, eventually, the relationship between gods and heroes, when humans start choosing their own fate assisted by the gods.

Hercules was the son of Zeus and Alkmene; the favourite hero of ancient Greeks. His twelve labors remain legendary.

Theseus was the son of King Aegeus; his greatest feat was killing the Minotaur following Ariadne's clue in the Minoan labyrinth.

Achilles was the greatest hero of the Iliad. He is remembered as the bravest Greek worrior in Troy as well as for the fact that he was invincible, except for his heel.

Perseus was the one who killed the mythical monster Medusa and rescued Andromeda. Hercules is his descendant.

Odysseus was the great Homeric hero. In the Iliad, he remained legendary and "resourceful" for coming up with the great idea of the Trojan Horse to conquer Troy and his adventures on his journey back to Ithaca, recorded in the other great Homeric epic, the Odyssey.

Bellerophon was the one who killed Chimera and owner of the mythical winged horse, Pegasus.

Dioscuri (Castor and Pollux) were twin brothers, sons of Zeus, who after their death became the constellation Gemini.

Jason was the leader of the Argonauts who fetched the Golden Fleece from Colchis.

OFFERINGS AND SACRIFICES

People, in an attempt to win the gods over, resorted to offerings in exchange for divine generosity and amity. Such offerings are known as sacrifices. Practicing these ritual of sacrifice had several goals, such as a good harvest, the validation of a sworn oath or alliance; the return of warriors from the battle.

The most common offering was animals – mainly oxen, bulls, rams, and sheep – which were ritually sacrificed on an altar. Priests, votaries, and animals approached the altar in a procession heading along the Iera Odos (Sacred Way). On arriving at the altar, the priest prayed to the gods with his arms raised toward heaven. Then, all together they would lead the animal on the altar to be sacrificed. After the sacrifice, the meat was grilled and eaten by the votaries, while the bones were thrown into the fire once more, still offered to the gods.

Nonetheless, there were bloodless sacrifices as well, also to favor the gods in return for the presents offered by votaries. Such rituals were libations, during which the votaries would pour a cup of wine, honey, olive oil, and water on the altar. Another offering was a "dekate" (tithe) with the votaries offering to the gods one tenth of their income that year; also, "aparche" (first fruits) involved the offering of the first crop or the first earnings.

THE WORLD OF THE DEAD

Nowadays, when someone dies, the relatives clothe and adorn the body before practicing the farewell rituals. Exactly the same was done in ancient Greece as well. After the burial, the relatives would honor the dead with libations, pouring oil and wine on the grave – a custom which remains today. Also, they would make the "polysporion", a mixture of cereal grains, currently called kollyva. Anyway, many of the contemporary rituals for the dead derive from the ancient Greek rituals. So, when someone left the world of the living, his or her family and friends would sit around and sing lament songs together as a congregation, for three days and three nights, just like nowadays. Also, the dead's favorite objects would be placed around the body in the tomb. In ancient Greece, the dead would be either buried or sometimes

Tomb

burned into the fire, depending on the era. However, ancient Greeks would put two coins (obols) on the eyes of the dead to pay the boatman ensuring safe passage through the Acheron River, in the Underworld.

WHAT ONE SHOULD KNOW ABOUT ANCIENT GREECE

LANGUAGE AND NUMBERS

Phoenicians were the people who invented the first alphabet; an alphabet with no symbols for vowels but only for consonants. The Greeks added symbols for vowels thus creating the first complete alphabet. Through the years, the letters kept changing until they acquired their current form.

The writing style was different. Nowadays, we write from left to right. Ancient Greeks originally wrote from right to left or even in lines alternately from right to left and vice versa. This resembled the lines on the ground made by the oxen when plowing a field; the specific writing style was called "boustrophedon" (ox-turning). Eventually, writing from left to right prevailed and continues up to present.

"Boustrophedon" writing style

THE MONTHS IN ANCIENT GREECE

Months had different names than the ones currently used; the latter being influenced by the Roman calendar. Also, each city-state had its own months – each one with a different name.

Ancient Greeks counted the years in Olympiads, that is based on the order of the Olympic Games. Thus, the first year of their calendar was 776 BC.

Hekatombaion	June 23 – July 23
Metageitnion	July 24 – August 22
Boedromion	August 23 – September 22
Pyanepsion	September 23 – October 22
Maimakterion	October 23 – November 22
Poseideon	November 23 – December 22
Gamelion	December 23 – January 22
Anthesterion	January 23 – February 20
Elaphebolion	February 21 – March 23
Mounichion	March 24 – April 22
Thargelion	April 23 – May 23
Skirophorion	May 24 – June 22

The months in the Athenian Calendar

PUBLIC ADMINISTRATION AND POLITICS

Athens in the 5th century BC might be a democracy, yet this was not always the case in the other city-states. Each city-state had its own regime, governing bodies, and justice authorities. For example, Sparta was a monarchy, Macedonia a kingship, while some cities of Asia Minor and the Peloponnese were tyrannies or aristocracies. Several city-states joined together in alliances to be safer in the event of war. Among the major alliances during that time were the Athenian and Peloponnesian Leagues. The members of an alliance were equal and had to help any allied city-state in need.

FAMILY AND SOCIETY

Family in Ancient Greece was a stage in a man's life towards becoming an active citizen. People formed families to have legitimate offspring and heirs to their property.

Wedding were actually a financial contract: always based on match-making and mainly on the dowry paid by the bride's parents. Ancient societies were primarily male dominated due to the prevailing lifestyle and contemporary needs.

Men dominated the family and society. Middle class men would pass their day at work, while the wealthy and nobles would pass their time discussing in the Agora (the market) or in philosophical schools. Their main role was to participate in public affairs, i.e. dealing with public administration. They had to supervise the work in the fields, as well as grocery shopping.

Women, on the other hand, led a rather different life. They would stay at home to raise their children and supervise slaves and housework. Their most common pastime was weaving on a loom, as well as teaching their daughters how to be proper wives and mothers. They would not take part in symposia or religious celebrations without being accompanied by their father or husband.

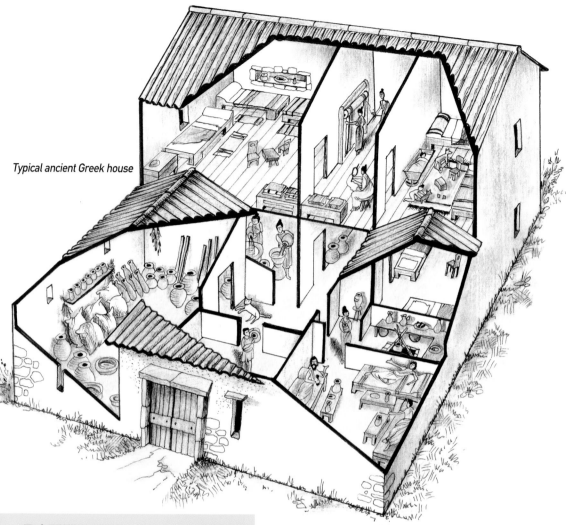

Typical ancient Greek house

DAILY LIFE

Every day men would have to go to work, go shopping for the house, and deal with the public affairs – the state. They would get up early and return home early too, as there were no lights in the streets at night. Women, on the other hand, would have to take care of the housework, go to the fountain to bring fresh water, and take care of their children.

People at that time led a simple life, regardless their social class. Their houses were small and similar to each other, so that no one could say whether a house belonged to a wealthy family or a poor family. Even the house of Pericles, the great leader of ancient Athens, was no different from the houses of any other ordinary citizen.

Typical andron (living room where only men entertained) — Classical era

FOOD

Their eating habits were simple as well: they cooked and had small meals of pretty much what modern Greeks currently eat. Their diet contained many cereals, legumes, vegetables, and fruits. They would often have meat meals, mostly beef and pork, while they were partial to game. They also liked seafood and shellfish. They used to have dairy products, especially cheese, plenty of honey, oil and wine, which they prefered watered down.

Of course, at the symposia and banquets of wealthy ancient Greeks, foods were luxurious and lavish.

ATTIRE

The materials with which they made their garments were natural: wool from animals, silk from silkworms,

Scene from a symposium, Attic red-figure kylix (480-470) London, British Museum

cotton and flax from plants. They would weave yarns on the looms to make fabrics to be sewed into very simple garments, worn in different ways. Of course, not all their clothes were white! Fabrics were dyed in natural dyes, while the rich would have their garments trimmed or elaborately embroidered!

Both men and women would wear the *himation* and the *chiton* (types of tunic).

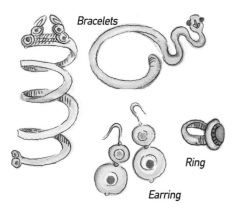
Bracelets

Ring

Earring

The women of wealthy families would wear jewelry: *earrings, necklaces, bracelets, pins*, and *brooches*. They were made of precious metals, gold, and beads, while masterfully elaborated by the ancient Greeks who were renouned silversmiths and goldsmiths. The jewels were kept in boxes, the *pyxis*, while cosmetics and perfumes used by women were kept in special vessels, the *alabastron*.

The robe was a long rectangular fabric sewed on the long sides and shoulders, forming sleeves, the cheirides, sewn or buttoned. A large belt called a zoster could be worn over the chiton.

A purely male garment was the chlamys; shorter than the chiton it was actually a piece of fabric draped over the right shoulder, covering the left arm.

The himation, was a long garment wrapped around the chest, under the left arm and tied on the shoulder.

The peplos (or Peplum) was a garment worn only by women. It was a rectangular piece of fabric longer than the height of the woman who wore it. This extra length of fabric could be draped on the back or chest and fastened over the shoulders and under the armpits. It was worn over the chiton. All clothes would be fastened with pins and brooches.

There were also several kinds of *hats*, as they are called nowadays.

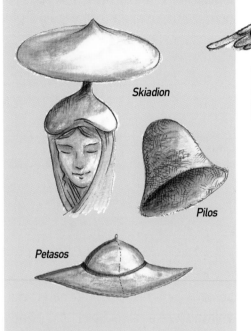

Skiadion

Pilos

Petasos

Finally, we should also mention the ancient Greek footwear, with best known the *sandals*, the *Krepides* and *endormis* or *emvas*.

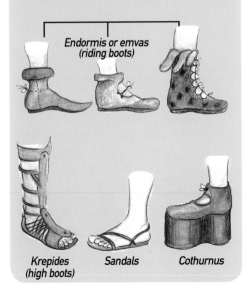

Endormis or emvas
(riding boots)

Krepides
(high boots)

Sandals

Cothurnus

PERSONAL HYGIENE

Personal hygiene was very important to ancient Greeks. Their homes featured a special place for bathing. It was a small room with vessels used to pour water on their bodies and natural sponges to rub themselves. After bathing, they would anoint their body with a mixture of olive oil and perfumes to keep their skin healthy.

Bathing was also one of the healing rituals in the temples of Asclepius to treat patients.

In the first large-scale installations, implemented in large sanctuaries, the water was cold, but in the 4th century BC the first thermal baths made their appearance.

EDUCATION

For boys...
In ancient Greece, all legal male children after the age of seven were educated by a teacher. The children of the rich could complete their

studies, while the poor ones could only learn how to read and write along with some craft to become professional workers or craftsmen. The coursebook of that era was the Homeric epics. They were also taught arithmetic and geometry, poetry and music. Advanced courses taught only to the rich included the dialectic, i.e the art of how to speak and express oneself correctly, astronomy and, of course, philosophy. If someone wished to follow a specific profession and become a physician, for instance, he had to become a student of a famous physician, to learn the science. Of course, ancient Greeks thought that only a healthy mind would not suffice if not accommodated in a healthy body. Thus, all students would train on a daily basis in running and wrestling.

...and girls

Once more, things were rather different for the girls... They stayed at home and learned from their mother how to sew, embroider, cook and do all housework. Of course, they learned how to write and read – always at home – but their basic task was to learn how to be obedient wives and good mothers.

Education of women in Sparta was different: women would train topless with the boys in order to build a strong and healthy body and thus give birth to strong children.

GAMES AND TOYS

Like all children nowadays, the children in ancient Greece had their own toys as well – almost identical to the modern ones!
Dolls! Is there a child that hasn't played with dolls or small pets? In ancient Greece small, brightly painted clay replicas of humans and animals were used. Some dolls had strings in their feet and hands so as to move. These dolls were called nevrospasta and are the first marionette puppets ever!

Nowadays, the sound of a rattle is used to relax a crying baby. Ancient Greeks as well, centuries ago, would use a *platage* or *platagon* (clay rattle), which was identical to the modern ones!

Children were also playing with the spintop, called *stromvos*, *strobilus* or *vemvix*.

The well known hide and seek, was called *apodidraskinda*; the blind man's buff is ancient Greek *Chalke Myia*, while *akinitinda* is our familiar game "who stirs first".

Children even currently hide something in their hand to have their friends guess in which is the full hand. Twenty-five centuries ago, children used to play the same game caled astragalizein.

Another children's game then was *Krikilasia* – using a metal rod to lead a wooden wheel to the height of their chest (currently 'tsiliki').

Neither board games are a modern invention! In ancient Greece, there were games with checkers. Among these, there was *"pentagrammon"* (Five Rows) similar to the modern Backgammon, in which the players had to move their checkers on five rows.

Of course, there were the *cubes* – the current dice. The best cast of the dice, the sixes, was called *"Aphrodite"* while the worst cast, the aces, was called *"the dog"*.

Ancient Greek toys and board games were usually made of clay or wood colored in natural dyes.

SPORTS

Running

Sport in Ancient Greece was particularly important. It was part of everyday life and essential for the education of young people.

The great sport events of antiquity, such as the four great Panhellenic games – the **Olympic, Pythian, Isthmian,** and **Nemean Games** – determined the course of sport in Greece and the whole world as well. The origin of these games dates back to the Rites of Passage, i.e. the coming-of-age ceremonies or in funeral games held in honor of the dead.

These events were divided into the following: i) running contests; ii wrestling contests; iii) equestrian events; iv) throw events; and v) jumping events.

i) Running contests included: the *stade race*, the *diaulos*, the *dolichos*, and *hoplitodromos*.

ii) Wrestling contests included: *boxing, wrestling* and *pankration*.

iii) Equestrian events included: *tethripon* (four-horse chariot race), *synoris* (two-horse chariot race) and *horse racing*.

iv) Throw events included: *discus* and *javelin throw*.

v) Last but not least, there was the pentathlon, which included: *running*, jump, *wrestling, javelin,* and *discus*.

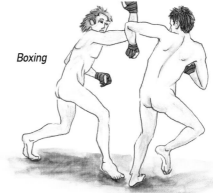

Boxing

Pankration

Chariot Racing

Discus Throw

Javelin Throw

Long Jump

Only long jump was performed, with the athletes running holding two weights – the dumbbells – to gain momentum.

All athletes competed naked. Before the event, they would leave their clothes in the locker room and rub their bodies with oil. When the events were over, they would go to the baths to wash. There they used a *sponge* and a special tool, the *strigil*, to remove the layer of oil, dust, and soil from their body.

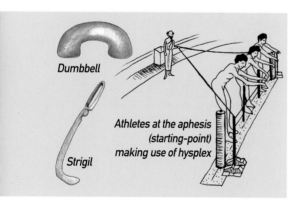

Dumbbell

Strigil

Athletes at the aphesis (starting-point) making use of hysplex

Every stadium and hippodrome featured a *starting line* as well as an *ysplix*, a system, positioned at the starting line, in front of the racers, to avoid early starts.

SLAVES

For ancient Greeks, slavery was perfectly normal. Every free citizen could have slaves in his possession, provided that he could afford and care for them. Slaves could belong to citizens, the state, and sanctuaries.

The status of slavery differs from city to city. Take, for example, two very well known, yet different city-states: Athens and Sparta.

In Athens, there were slaves belonging to the state and others belonging to citizens, who could do with them whatever they wanted, for instance, to resell them.

In Sparta, the slaves were called *helots* and belonged to the State. Citizens could use them, but they had no right to resell them.

The main source of slaves was war. The defeated would be arrested, allocated as war trophies to the victors or sold in the Agora (the market) of each city. Any travelers seized by pirates were also sold as slaves. Moreover, the children of slaves would be slaves as well. Often, those who could not repay their debts would become slaves to their lenders as a way of repayment.

The living conditions of the slaves depended on their owner. They lived in the homes they worked, together with their owners, where they dinned and participated in festivals and sacrifices. There were also the pedagogues, the slaves who accompanied children to school and other educational activities. They often had friendly relations with their owners. Of course, there were many cases of slave punishment. However, there are also several cases of citizens being punished because they wronged or mistreated or even exercised violence upon slaves. Finally, slaves could purchase their freedom and become freedmen, either by giving to their owner the amount he had paid to buy them or showing bravery and valor in battle.

IN THE WAR

For ancient Greeks war was part of their everyday life. It was an inevitable evil, which nonetheless acquired heroic dimensions.

Ancient Greeks wore brass armor made to protect their chest and back. Their weapons were the *sword*, the *spear*, the *bow*, and the *shield*, used not only to protect their body, but also to push the opponent (othismos).

They would fight in a *phalanx*, i.e. standing side by side, with their spears towards the enemy. The most important thing about the phalanx was that they were all

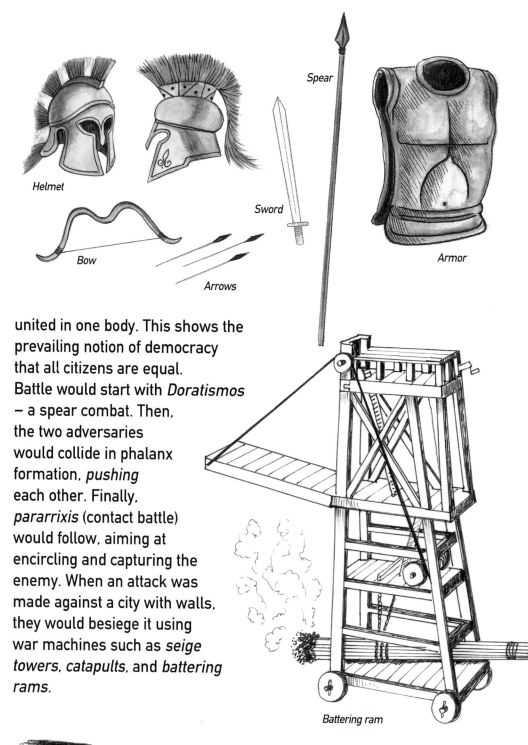

Helmet

Bow

Arrows

Sword

Spear

Armor

united in one body. This shows the prevailing notion of democracy that all citizens are equal. Battle would start with *Doratismos* – a spear combat. Then, the two adversaries would collide in phalanx formation, *pushing* each other. Finally, *pararrixis* (contact battle) would follow, aiming at encircling and capturing the enemy. When an attack was made against a city with walls, they would besiege it using war machines such as *seige towers*, *catapults*, and *battering rams.*

Battering ram

Battering ram with a bronze head

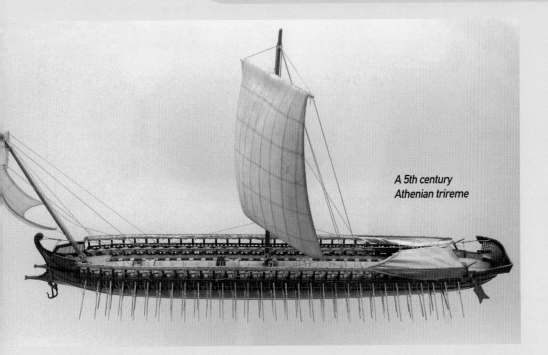

A 5th century Athenian trireme

Of course, there were sea battles as well. The Athenians had the best navy of the time. The largest ancient warships were the triremes, with three banks of oars one below the other. They were light and nimble ships that could travel at high speeds.

The bravery and courage of the Greeks in the battle has been praised by several scholars, politicians, even by their own opponents! This is because they never fought for anyone's interests, but only in defense of their homeland. Anyway, ancient Greeks themselves believed that:

"...your country is more precious and more to be revered and is holier and in higher esteem among the gods and among men of understanding than your mother and your father and all your ancestors, ..." [Socrates (Plato, Criton 51a, 51b)]

«ΜΗΤΡΟΣ ΤΕ ΚΑΙ ΠΑΤΡΟΣ ΚΑΙ ΤΩΝ ΑΛΛΩΝ ΠΡΟΓΟΝΩΝ ΑΠΑΝΤΩΝ ΤΙΜΙΩΤΕΡΟΝ ΕΣΤΙΝ Η ΠΑΤΡΙΣ ΚΑΙ ΣΕΜΝΟΤΕΡΟΝ ΚΑΙ ΑΓΙΩΤΕΡΟΝ ΚΑΙ ΕΝ ΜΕΙΖΟΝΙ ΜΟΙΡΑ ΚΑΙ ΠΑΡΑ ΘΕΟΙΣ ΚΑΙ ΠΑΡ' ΑΝΘΡΩΠΟΙΣ ΤΟΙΣ ΝΟΥΝ ΕΧΟΥΣΙ».

ARTS, ENTERTAINMENT AND SCIENCES

ARCHITECTURE

The finest and grandest buildings in ancient Greece were created in the Classical period. The material used was marble. The monuments of Athens are built of Pentelic marble; yet equally famous marbles were those of Paros and Naxos.

Quarry workers mined the marble into giant pieces and cut it into smaller slabs. Then, with the help of animals and carts, these slabs were transported to the construction site. There, hammers, saws, and chisels were used to bring the marble to its final form. The finished marble slabs were hoisted into place with ropes and cranes. Finally, they were fastened together with metal rods.

Columns supported the upper part of the temple which the *capital* – the piece on top – decorated. The columns support a large horizontal section called the *architrave*, on which the *frieze* lies; the frieze supports a large triangular piece, the *pediment*. At the time, there were two main orders of architecture – two different ways of building – the *Doric* and the *Ionic* order, with no major differences between them. The Ionic order is more refined and elegant than the Doric, which is heavier and more imposing. Their main differences, however, are that Ionic *capitals* are decorated with two circular volutes, the *helices*, and the columns have bases, while the Doric capitals are almost rectangular and the columns have no bases at all.

Another difference is that the Ionic frieze is a single piece, while the Doric one is separated by vertical channels, the

Doric Column

Ionic Column

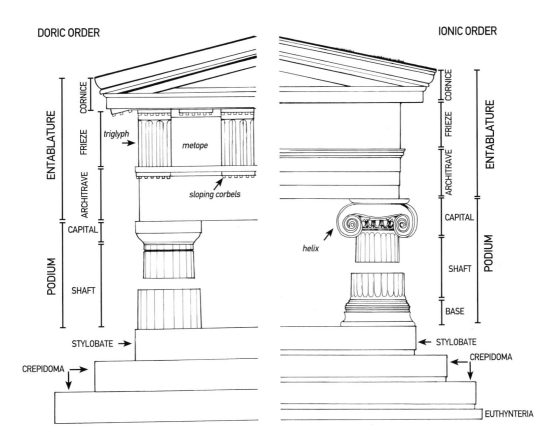

DORIC ORDER

ENTABLATURE
- CORNICE
- FRIEZE — *triglyph* — *metope*
- ARCHITRAVE — *sloping corbels*

PODIUM
- CAPITAL
- SHAFT

STYLOBATE →

CREPIDOMA →

IONIC ORDER

ENTABLATURE
- CORNICE
- FRIEZE
- ARCHITRAVE

PODIUM
- CAPITAL — *helix*
- SHAFT
- BASE

← STYLOBATE

CREPIDOMA

EUTHYNTERIA

triglyphs, in between which are spaces, called *metopes*.

Later, another order was developed, the *Corinthian order*, its main feature being far more ornate capitals, than the Ionic, with embossed floral decoration.

The inside of temples were divided into three sections: the *vestibule* or *narthex*, the *nave*, where the statue

Corinthian Capital

of the god was placed, and the *opisthodome*.

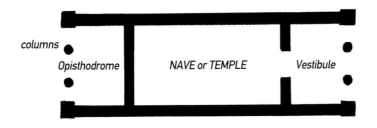

columns

Opisthodrome   NAVE or TEMPLE   Vestibule

SCULPTURE

Ancient Greece is renouned for its beautiful sculptures; they are everywhere: in temples, cemeteries, libraries, theaters… There were marble and bronze statues, busts and relief sculptures carved on one side only standing out from a background surface.

If a maker wanted to make a marble statue, bust, or relief, he would buy a big piece of marble in the preferable size. Then, he would use his tools to remove material from the surface giving the marble its form. Thus, small parts from a big piece of marble were removed until it acquired the form he wanted. With drills, needles, chisels, and other tools he could achieve the surface details.

Now, if he had to create a bronze statue, there were two options depending, of course, on its size. For small-scale statues, bronze was melted and cast into a mold – a casing, made of two pieces of clay, each one in the form of each side of the work. Once the metal has cooled, the work of art was liberated by carefully breaking the mold. Large-scale statues were first cast in several pieces – the individual parts of the intended statue – and then were connected together and had the seams smoothed.

Of course, there were also clay figurines, the *idols*, but they were usually rather small. The craftsman would create the figurine with a piece of clay, usually with his hands, and then he would paint it if he wanted and finally bake it. Clay figurines might not be of the same value as the other sculptures, but they were very beautiful and well made.

As expected, there were many famous sculptors who would take orders from people, sanctuaries, and the city-states. Among them were **Phidias**, **Praxiteles**, **Myron**, and **Polykleitos**.

POTTERY

The most common objects in ancient Greece were vessels. There were two types of vessels: *utilitarian* and *luxury*.

Utilitarian vessels were those commonly used by people in everyday life, for cooking or transport and storage of several products.

Luxury vessels were mostly used as gifts, prizes for competitions, offerings to the gods, or to display at the houses of the wealthy.

Utilitarian vessels were usually very simply decorated, while luxury ones were sumptuous and sometimes even gold plated!

Angiography – the drawing of the vessel – was either *melanomorpha* (black-figure) or *erythromorfa* (red-figure). Melanomorpha is the oldest style with the figures painted black, while in red-figure ceramic painting the figures are painted red. The vessels were usually decorated with anthropomorphic and geometric designs, animals, plants and fish. Luxury vessels depicted complete representations, such as battle scenes, shipwrecks, religious processions, and mythological incidents.

The vessels are divided in two further categories, depending on the shape of their neck: the lidded or closed and the open vessels. Lidded vessels are those with a small neck, used for liquids, while open vessels were those with a large opening, used for solid foods and objects. There were several types of vessels, each with its own name.

33

Calyx krater

Oinochoe

Stamnos

Amphora

Amphora

Pelike

Hydria

Loutrophorus

Lekythos

Loutrophorus

Volute krater

Kantharos

Cotyl

Kylix

PAINTING

Painting is a very important part of ancient Greek art. Many buildings of that era were decorated with paintings and frescoes, but unfortunately only few have survived.

Kore No. 675.
Acropolis
Museum

For example, the north hall of the Propylaea of the Acropolis is known as the Pinakotheke ("Gallery"), because it housed paintings by famous artists of the era, such as the painter **Polygnotos**.

The Pompeion at the Kerameikos Cemetery was also decorated with frescoes. Contemporary writers said it accommodated the portraits of tragedians.

Among the most important frescos to survive until modern times are in the Royal Tombs of Vergina, including the tomb of Philip II, Alexander the Great's father. These frescoes were found both inside and outside the tomb and represented hunting and chariot race scenes, as well as the abduction of Persephone.

Another building of the era decorated with frescoes is the Treasury of the Cnide in Delphi. These frescoes were also created by Polygnotos. Their artistic value was so great that Attalus II, the king of Pergamum, sent painters to restore them.

However, it is important to keep in mind that all marble sculptures – even those adorning buildings and temples – were colored instead of white as we currently see them! They were brightly painted in red, blue, brown and yellow dye. Even today there are sculptures with their color preserved; so we can imagine how they were when created.

diaulos

aulos

syrinx

cymbals

cithara

pnitis (trigonon)

phorminx

lyre

barbiton

MUSIC

Ancient Greek music instruments are divided into three main categories: the *cordophones*, i.e. those with strings; the *aerophones*, i.e. those who make sound when blown; and the *membranophones*, i.e. percussion instruments which make sound when they are hit.

The most famous stringed musical instrument were the *lyre*, the *phorminx*, the *cithara*, and the *barbitos*. They were quite similar except in the number of chords and their size. They were played with the help of a plectrum (made of horns, wood, bone or metal), rather than the fingers.

Another stringed instrument was the *trigonon* or *pnitis*, much like a modern harp, which is played with the fingers.

Wind instruments were the *aulos*, the *syrinx*, and the *salpinx*.

The aulos was much like modern flute. It was a long tube with holes, which the musician covered with his fingers to make the sound he wanted. The aulos could be single or double, called *diaulos*.

The *syrinx* (or pan flute) was made of reed pipes tied together with wax and flax with vertical supports. Finally, the *salpinx* was a long tube with small openings at their base much like modern trumpet.

The main percussion instruments were the *tympanum*, the *cymbals*, and the *sistrum*. The tympanum was similar to the current hand drum; the cymbals were small metal discs hit together; and the sistrum resembled modern baby rattles.

POETRY

For ancient Greek, poetry was entertainment, learning, and a way to express their feelings. Poems were recited at banquets and celebrations, in the market, or were used as textbooks in schools.

Ancient Greek poetry is divided into the *epic, dramatic,* and *lyric* genres. By epic poetry, we mean the great poems narrating heroic deeds of the past. Originally, they were recited accompanied by the phorminx and later without any music; only the expression of the Rhapsodist. The most famous epic poems are **Homer's** epics: the *Iliad* and the *Odyssey*.

Dramatic poetry is intended for theatrical performance by actors on the stage. It includes tragedy,

comedy, and the satyr play. The parts of dramatic poetry accompanied by music were sung by a chorus, while the actors only recited.

Homer

Lyric differ from the dramatic and epic poems because they are shorter and refer to people's everyday life, passions, and emotions; they are always recited accompanied by music.

Lyric poetry is divided into categories according to the number of performers, i.e. people who recited the poems accompanied by music. So, lyric poetry is divided into two distinct media of performance: *monody* (solo song) and *choral lyric* (also known as choral odes); the former with a single performer, while the latter with a group of performers. Choral odes were further subdivided into other gernes, depending on whether they were dedicated to gods or humans. Some of the lyric poetry themes were human emotions and destiny, natural world, society, and politics.

Some great lyric poets were **Archilochus**, **Solon**, **Sappho**, and **Pindar**.

Pindar

PROSE

Prose is written work without any rules or measure, but is rather in the form of text.

The oldest prose ever written and saved in its complete form is the *History of Herodotus.* **Herodotus** was born in 485 BC in Halicarnassus, Caria and died in 425 BC in Thurii, southern Italy. His writings are about the "Median affair". His work is based on reliable sources, making clear the true causes of the events described. It is the first historical text and this is why Herodotus is called *Father of History.*

Then, there is the great **Thucydides**. He was born in Alimos, Attica, in 455 BC and died in 399 BC. His work recounts the events of the Peloponnesian War and more specifically, the years

Thucydides

between 21 and 27 BC. He is the first one who worked as a modern historian. The information provided is accurate as he visited and described the battlefields himself and studied official records and documents. Thucydides' work, i.e. the narration of the events of the Peloponnesian War after 411 BC, was continued by **Xenophon**. He was born in Athens in 430 BC and died in 355 BC. He wrote several philosophical and didactic works, as well as the first historical novel, *the Anabasis Kyrou*

Xenophon

(The Expedition of Cyrus). As a historian he could not reach the grandeur of Thucydides, nonetheless he is a good source of information.

All three above mentioned authors wrote history. However, there was another writer as well who was very famous for his short fables... Aesop!

Aesop

Aesop lived in the 6th century BC and is said to be a freedman slave from Samos. He had travelled much and met many different peoples. Through his fables, where animals talk and think just like people, Aesop teaches the value of goodness and virtue, in a pleasant and fun way.

DRAMA AND THEATRE

One of the favorite entertainments for ancient Greeks was drama. In the ancient Greek theatre it didn't matter if you were rich or poor, a man, a woman or a child; there were seats for everybody.

Ancient Greek theaters were originally wooden, but later they were made of marble. What's most remarkable is that then the theaters were so large that they could accommodate audiences of thousands; and while there were no microphones, the actors could be perfectly heard even to the spectator sitting in the last tier!

In ancient plays, often a mekane (machine) was used for the appearances of the gods onto the stage. This god appeared to

We will describe an ancient theater, starting from the Skene (stage): It was a large rectangular building behind the orchestra, which was used as the modern backstage dressing rooms. In front of the skene there was the proskenion, an originally wooden columnade. Among the columns there were doors and the settings. In front of the stage, there was logeion, an elevated platform where the actors were performing. On both sides of the stage and proskenion there were two lanes, the parodoi, which ended in the orchestra, the large semicircular space where the chorus performed. In the center of the orchestra there was the Thymeli, the altar of Dionysus. Then, there was the koilon, the semi-circular construction of tiered seats intended for the audience. Koilon, is subdivided into several parts. The most important part was the kerkis, the seats of the spectators. The front seats were called Proedria and were reserved for officials and priests. Kerkis was divided in two diazoma, the upper and the lower one, the horizontal semicircular corridors and the klimax, vertical steps for the spectators to reach their seats.

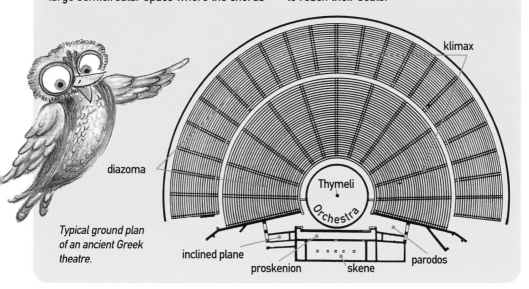

Typical ground plan of an ancient Greek theatre.

klimax

diazoma

Thymeli

Orchestra

inclined plane

proskenion

skene

parodos

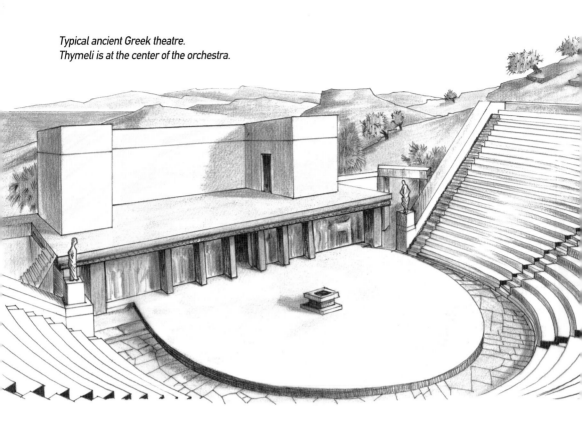

Typical ancient Greek theatre.
Thymeli is at the center of the orchestra.

descend on the stage from heaven, just when time was right to save someone or give a solution. This invention of the ancient Greeks coined the expression "*deus ex machina*" that we use today.

At that time, all the roles – even women's – were performed by male actors. They would dress up according to the needs of the play and put on the *cothurnus* (see page 22), special shoes with very high soles to make them look taller and more imposing to the viewers. Finally, all actors wore masks to avoid showing their faces. These masks were made to show only the feelings and quality of the character.

Ancient Greek drama was of three types: *tragedy*, the *satyr play* and *comedy*.

Tragedy was the representation of events accompanied by music and chorus. In the parts of the play where action took place, words were spoken by the actors; music parts were performed by the chorus. Tragedy aimed to produce powerful emotions in the audience such as sadness, anger, shame, anxiety, and fear, in order to make

Ancient theatre masks

them understand the events happening on stage. The most renouned tragic poets were **Aeschylus**, **Sophocles,** and **Euripides**.

The satyr play was a comic play that aimed to entertain the spectators after tragic experiences. It always had a happy ending and usually made fun of mythological events, or even tragedies already staged.

The comedy was meant to entertain the audience with its humoristic plot. Through humor, the poet satirized and criticized society, politicians, significant locals, even other poets, regardless their grandeur. The most important and well-known comic poet to date, and father of satire, is **Aristophanes**!

Some of the most famous theaters of the time were those of *Dionysus* in Athens, *Epidaurus* (used even today), *Oropos, Eretria, Thorikus, Piraeus,* and *Megalopolis.*

Aeschylus   *Sophocles*   *Euripides*   *Aristophanes*

TREATMENT AND MEDICINE

Ancient Greeks had made great advances in medicine just as in any other science. They prepared herbal medicines, used medical instruments almost identical to the modern ones, and performed particularly difficult and complex surgeries. The patron god of medicine was Asclepius, while the greatest physician of antiquity and founder of ancient and modern medicine was Hippocrates.

Asclepius

Asclepius was said to be the mortal son of Apollo and the nymph Coronis. According to legend, he was brought up by the centaur Chiron, who taught him the art of medicine. Asclepius became a healing deity who cured people of their illness through enkoimesis (i.e. incubation). He appeared to the sleeping votaries during their stay in the sanctuary showing them the right treatment.

The priests of Asclepius taught the art of medicine in his sanctuaries and helped patients. Sanctuaries of Asclepius were found in Athens, Piraeus, Trikala, and Kos.

Hippocrates

Hippocrates was born in Kos in 460 BC and is considered the father of modern medicine. His father descended from Asclepius and the clan of his mother from Hercules. After his studies he started working as a physician in Kos, but soon decided to travel and teach the science of medicine to others. In his travels he healed many people and saved many cities from plague. He died in Larissa at the age of 83, in 377 BC. His legacy was the *Hippocratic collection*, a total of 59 medical research texts, lectures and philosophical essays on medicine, taught even today. The Hippocratic medicine was very strict and physicians who practiced it were renowned throughout the world as the best surgeons!

In all modern universities around the world, young physicians on graduation still swear the *Hippocratic Oath*, the very text first written by the great physician of antiquity in the 4th century BC.

Centaur

SCIENCES

Ancient Greeks developed all sciences, i.e. geometry, mathematics, astronomy, physics and engineering, to a great extent. Many wise people of the time dealt with these disciplines, wrote books, stipulated theories and laws applicable up to present, and taught in schools and universities. They built complex machines, invented ways of measuring, predicted eclipses, created laws and theories of music, discovered the structure of atoms, and tried to explain the creation of the world.
Some of the most important scientists of ancient Greece were: **Thales of Miletus**, **Euclid**, **Democretus**, **Anaximenes**, **Anaxinader**, **Heraclitus**, **Pythagoras** and **Archimedes**.

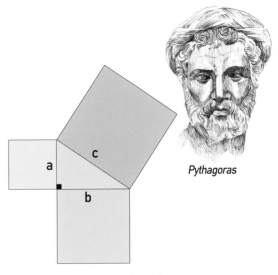
Pythagoras

PYTHAGOREAN THEOREM
$$a^2 + b^2 = c^2$$

Democretus

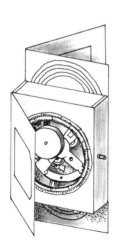
Representation of the "Antikythera Mechanism"; It was discovered in 1900 in a shipwreck near the isle of Antikythera and is considered the forerunner of the modern computer. (National Archaeological Museum of Athens)

The "Aeolopyle of Heron"; the first steam machine in history.

"The Dove" or "petomichani" a flying machine invented by Archytas; The first jet in history, forerunner of the modern airplane.

ANCIENT ATHENS

DEMOCRACY AND INSTITUTIONS

It is well known that democracy was born in Greece and more specifically in Athens. After several political systems, such as the aristocracy, kingship, monarchy, and tyranny, the citizens of Athens in the 5th century BC created the first democracy, which constituted the basis of all subsequent democracies around the world.

DEMOCRACY

What we currently call democracy, is rather different from the democracy of ancient Athens... of course, there are common characteristics between the two political systems, such as government of, by and for the people, equality of all citizens, and judicial independence. In ancient Athens, however, the power of the people was immediate, i.e. people themselves, without any representatives such as current MPs, would draft and vote about the state laws. This means that the citizens were the state and the state was the citizens. Also, all adult Athenians had the right to participate in state governance.

Ecclesia of Demos

The most important institution of the Athenian state was that of the *Ecclesia of Demos;* demos meaning people in ancient Greek. It was the body of all Athenian citizens which instituted laws, the Supreme Court, and the top of state government. Each citizen could propose and vote about laws.

Council of 500

This political body comprised by 50 citizens elected by lot from each of the 10 tribes of Athens. Their role was to process the laws proposed by the Ecclesia of Demos and to undertake public administration.

COURTS

The courts were created to observe compliance with the laws and punishment of wrongdoers. Ecclesia of Demos was the Supreme Court, followed by Areopagus and jury courts. All court

Lots

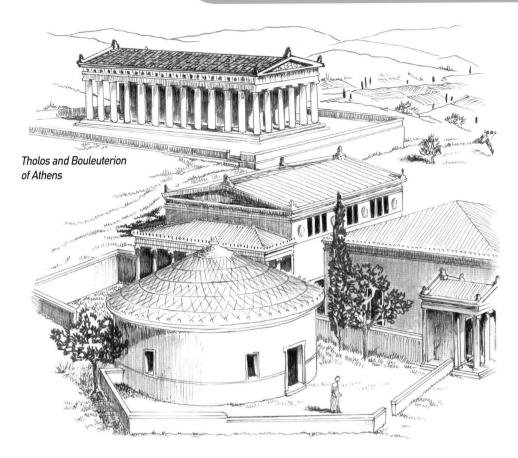

*Tholos and Bouleuterion
of Athens*

members were ordinary citizens elected by lot. The penalties imposed were fine, exile, disenfranchisement, confiscation of property, and even death, depending of course on the offense.

BOARD OF 10 GENERALS

Another institution of the Athenian state was the *Board of 10 Generals.* They were elected by vote from the upper classes and had their eligibility assessed by test. Their competence comprised army administration and logistical

support relating to war campaigns. The term of their office was annual and, unlike other offices of the government, they could be re-elected as many times as they wanted.

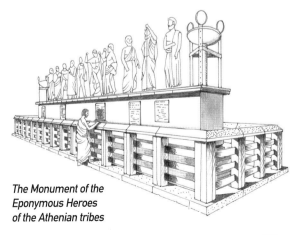

*The Monument of the
Eponymous Heroes
of the Athenian tribes*

OSTRACISM

The Athenians, in an attempt to protect their democracy, created the institution of *ostracism*.
Each citizen, on establishing that someone was trying to overrule democracy and become a tyrant, would carve on an osktakon – a hard piece of clay – the name and father's name of the person considered dangerous. Then, the citizens counted the pieces and if someone's name was written on 6,000 of them, he was banished from the city for 5 or 10 years. Ostracism was respected by all citizens, regardless their origin.
For the Athenians, democracy was sacred and often sacrificed their lives to protect it. Anyway, democracy is one of the greatest gifts of the ancient Athenian culture to the future generations of the whole world...

One day, the Athenian general Aristides, son of Lysimachus was walking around the Agora when a passerby stopped him. Without knowing who he was talking to, he asked Aristides to write for him on an ostrakon the name of the man who wanted to be exiled, as he was illiterate. Aristides asked him who this man was only to listen to the man saying: "General Aristides". Without saying anything, he wrote his name on the piece of clay, gave it to the man, thanked him and continued his way. Aristides was exiled in 484/483 BC to Aegina and was called Aristides the just ever since, because he respected democracy and the opinion of a simple man. Even currently, in the museum of Ancient Agora there are ostraka with his name on them.

PHILOSOPHY AND EDUCATION

In Athens of the 5th century BC probably the most significant events in the history of world civilization occurred. Democracy was established, great monuments were created and human thought, philosophy, and sciences were developed as never before. Democracy assisted greatly to such flourishing with liberty of speech and especially the emergence of enlightened men, the philosophers, who taught freely in the Agora or the schools they founded. The most important ones were Socrates, Plato, and Aristotle.

Socrates was born in 470/469 BC in Athens. He was the son of Sofroniscus, a sculptor, and Faenerete, a midwife. He was very ugly and walked around barefoot

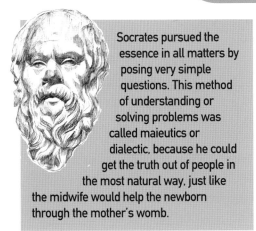

Socrates pursued the essence in all matters by posing very simple questions. This method of understanding or solving problems was called maieutics or dialectic, because he could get the truth out of people in the most natural way, just like the midwife would help the newborn through the mother's womb.

Plato was born in 429/428 BC in Athens. He came from a wealthy and aristocratic family and received the appropriate education. At the age of 20 he met 63-year old Socrates and became his student for the next eight years. Some years after Socrates' death, he founded the renowned Academy in Athens. It was the first of its kind and precursor of all modern universities. Most philosophers who lived after Plato were either his students or attended his Academy. The Academy of Plato was closed in

wearing his single robe. He soon acquired numerous students and his speech would fascinate his audience. Socrates said that man must first of all get to know himself and the meaning of politics and ethics in society. In 399 BC, he was accused of blasphemy, allegedly to "teach of new demons" in the city. Socrates meant that he was introducing a new way of thinking, but his opponents deliberately misinterpreted his words, maintaining that he wanted to introduce new gods. He was charged of it, tried, judged guilty and eventually sentenced to death. Socrates, without any protest accepted the sentence imposed to die by drinking hemlock, a powerful poison, remaining faithful to the laws of the city and himself – actually putting his teachings to practice.

Plato was well known for his Theory of Ideas (or Theory of Forms), according to which the world is divided into two parts: what is perceived through our senses and what actually exists, but we perceive only through mind and truth. Based on this theory, Plato planned his Ideal State, in which every citizen had a role depending on their knowledge and education. In this state, people are divided into classes according to their education rather than their financial status.

529 AD after nine centuries of operation. Plato died in Athens in 347 BC.

Aristotle

Aristotle was born in 384 BC in Stagira of Chalkidiki. In 367 BC, at the age of 17, he came to Athens and studied at the Academy of Plato. He stayed with the Academy for 20 years – first as a student and then as a teacher.

After his travels in Asia Minor, he arrived in Macedonia where he was invited by King Philip II to undertake the education of the successor to the throne, Alexander the Great. Aristotle taught young Alexander the *Iliad*, the *Odyssey*, as well as the works of the great tragedians. On completing his work in Macedonia, he returned to Athens and founded his own school, the *Lyceum*. Aristotle defined philosophy as an attempt to interpret nature and dealt with several other subjects apart from philosophy. He died in Chalkidiki, in 322 BC.

RHETORIC

When a citizen would be tried for an offense, he would hire someone to help him be acquitted. So, he hired someone like a current lawyer. That time, this was the task of the orators, who wrote the defendants' apologies. They would also speak at the Agora, attempting to influence public opinion. The major ancient Greek orators came from Attica.

Antiphon was born in about 485 BC at Rhamnus in Attica. He was the first to write down his speeches and the first who adapted rhetoric to the courts. He died in 410 BC drinking poison hemlock.

Andocides was born in Athens in 440 BC. He was pro-oligarch and belonged to the aristocratic class. He died away from Athens – unknown when.

Lysias, one of the greatest orators of antiquity was born in Athens in 445 BC. He wrote more than 230 orations but unfortunately only 34 survived completed. He died in Athens in 380 BC.

Isocrates was born in Athens in 436 BC. He was a teacher of

Lysias

Isocrates

Aeschines

Demosthenes

rhetoric; he wrote very important orations and was a supporter of Philip II, the king of Macedonia. He died in Athens in 338 BC.

Isaeos was born in Chalkis in 420 BC and was a student of Isocrates. Ancient critics called him a pettifogger, because he could adapt laws and facts to serve his purpose. He died around 350 BC.

Hypereides was born in Athens in 390 BC. He was a general and politician opposed to the hegemony of King Philip II. He was killed by the Macedonian general Antipater in 322 BC.

Lycurgus was born in Athens in 390 BC. He studied at the Academy of Plato and later he became a student of Isocrates. He was very austere and proposed the death penalty for anyone who didn't do his duty towards his country. He died in 324 BC.

Aeschines was born in Athens in 390 BC and fought against the Thirty Tyrants. He was the first to speak about the Macedonian expansionism, which he was opposed to. He died in 330 BC.

Demosthenes was born in 385 BC in Athens. He was a student of Isocrates and Isaeos and the greatest orator of antiquity. He was divested from his fortune by his relatives and had to write oratories to make his living – about 60 in total. He tried to make a speech to the Ecclesia of Demos but he was lisper and nobody would listen to him. So, he practiced on his own and managed to correct his problem. He was also anti-Macedonian and in opposition to Isocrates about this issue. He was sentenced to exile accused of bribery; and when once he returned to Athens, he had to fly away anew chased by the Antipater. He took refuge in the temple of Poseidon in Poros, where he was eventually found by the soldiers. There, he committed suicide drinking poison to avoid arrest.

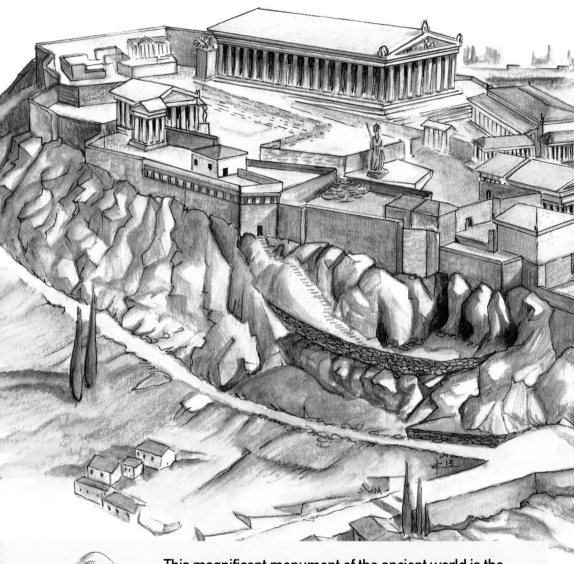

Περικλής

This magnificent monument of the ancient world is the symbol of the city of Athens. It is the splendid creation of the cooperation of three artists: the architects Iktinos and Kallikratis and the sculptor Phidias. The initiative for the construction and renovation of the buildings of the rock of Acropolis belongs to the ruler of the city, the great Pericles, who ruled Athens in the 5th century BC the so called *"Golden Age of Pericles"*.

A copy of the golden and ivory statue of Athena in the temple of Parthenon made by Phidias; National Archaeological Museum of Athens

To enter the main area of the Acropolis, you have to pass the *Propylaia*, a large a flight of stairs with rooms on the right and left. The left room housed the Pinakothek, which accommodated works of the great painter Polygnotus. This was the first gallery (= pinakothek in Greek) in the world. Unfortunately, the Propylaea were never completed; and this was because of the *Peloponnesian War* between the Athenians and the Spartans that broke out.

As you pass the Propylaea on your right, there is the Temple of Athena Nike. It was completely demolished by the Turks when they conquered Greece, but most pieces were saved so reconstruction was possible.

Now you are on the rock. The temple you see on your left is the *Erechtheion*. It is an oblong temple with 6 columns on the east side. It features a grand entrance portico on the north side while the south

Erechtheion

Korai: archaic marble
standing draped
female figures

features a covered area with its roof supported by Korai, known as the *Caryatids*. In this temple the goddess Athena along with the heroes and mythical kings of ancient Athens were worshiped. Actually, in the back of the temple – the western part – tradition says it is the site of the sacred olive tree, Athena's gift to the city. On the right of the Erechtheion there was the great bronze statue of Athena Promachos, Phidias' work, approximately 13 meters high, which unfortunately has been lost. The whole space among the temples was filled with statues and inscriptions, all dedicated to goddess Athena from the votaries and pilgrims. Many of them are now housed in the new Acropolis Museum.

Finally, the masterpiece of ancient Greek art: the Parthenon. Its construction began in 447 BC and ended in 438 BC.

It is surrounded by 8 columns at either end and 17 on the long sides, while the great sculptor Phidias with his apprentices adorned the whole temple with beautiful sculptures:
The metopes depicted scenes from the Battle of the Centaurs, of the Giants, of the Amazons, as well as the fall of Troy.
The frieze of the temple depicts the Panathenaic procession, the great festivity of the city in honor of goddess Athena.
On the pediments, the birth of Athena and her conflict with Poseidon, over who would become the patron of the city.
Inside the temple, there was the big chryselephantine statue of Athena Parthenos – which is not saved – also Phidias' creation. It was 10 meters high! The goddess is depicted standing, holding a Nike in her right hand and a shield in the left, and the serpent, her sacred symbol, lying beside her.

East pediment of the Parthenon

Many of the Parthenon sculptures were stolen by the Englishman Lord Elgin, while Greece was conquered by the Turks. Workers with saws and hammers broke sculptures to pieces, thus destroying the temple, to be easily shipped to England. Eighteen statues from the pediments, fifteen metopes, one Caryatid and 246 feet of frieze are now being exhibited in the British Museum.

PANATHENAEA

The Panathenaea festival was dedicated to goddess Athena, the patron of the city. It was the most glamorous religious and sport event held every summer in mid-August. In 556 BC, Peisistratus, the tyrant of Athens reorganized the festivities and added sport events equal to the standards of the Olympic Games, thus establishing the Greater Panathenaea. It was comprised of sports competitions, music, rhapsody, ie recitating epic poems such as Homer's epics, and drama contests were also comprised. The festival was divided into two parts. The first one included sport events in which athletes from all cities participated, while the second, included sports and dances derived from the mythological traditions of the city. In these events, only Athenian athletes could participate. In the Panathenaea, winners would be awarded with the famous Panathenaic amphorae filled with oil from the sacred olive trees of the city, money, as well as golden and olive wreaths. The most important event of the festivities was, of course, the Panathenaic Procession which was held on the birthday of goddess Athena, on August 28th. All Athenians, as well as delegates from other cities, ambassadors and official guests participated in the procession. The priests led the procession accompanying the Panathenaic ship on wheels. From its mast the

competitions in Panathenaea

olive

The Panathenaic procession as depicted on the frieze on the north side of the Parthenon. The offering of the sacred veil is represented in the middle

embroidered veil for goddess Athena – woven for nine months by maids from noble families of the city – was hanging like a sail.

The procession would start from the *Pompeion*, a building of Kerameikos, crossed the Panathenaic Way, passing through the Ancient Agora and then ended on the rock of Acropolis. There, the sacred veil was put on the wooden statue of goddess Athena in Erechtheion. Finally, the great carnage *ecatombe* took place – the sacrifice of 100 oxen on the great altar. After sacrifice, the meat was grilled and eaten by the votaries. The Panathenaic festival was abandoned in 426 AD by order of the Emperor Theodosius, after a long period of decline ever since the establishment of Christianity, when people stopped believing in the twelve Olympians.

DIONYSUS AND DRAMATIC COMPETITIONS

The Panathenaea was indeed the biggest festival in Athens; yet, another major celebration was the Greater or City Dionysia. It was introduced by the tyrant Pisistratus of Athens in the mid 6th century BC, in honor of the god Dionysus, who was the patron of drama, and featured the biggest dramatic competition in Greece. It was held from 8 to 13 of the Athenian month Elaphebolion, that is late March to early April, and lasted six days. Venue of the competition was the theater of Dionysus at the foot of the rock of Acropolis. Its current form is the Roman one, as the Romans renovated the theater and added the marble thrones and embossed facade depicting scenes from Dionysus' life.

Responsible for the organization of the festival was the eponymous archon, who chose the richest Athenians to be sponsors and fund the group of artists who would participate in the dramatic competitions. In addition, the state would pay an amount to the poor citizens, "*theoric*" or Theoric Fund, so they could afford their ticket to watch the performances.

On the first day of the festival there were sacrifices, processions and ceremonies in honor of the god Dionysus and the following day the dramatic competitions would start. The winner – poet and the sponsor were crowned with wreaths of ivy, the sacred plant of the god Dionysus. The sponsor, who had financed the play, could have a monument built to his victory. This monument was called the Choragic Monument and was placed at the street of Tripods. Finally, apart from the Greater Dionysia there were also the Lesser or Rural Dionisia as well. They were held in the second half of the month of Poseideion in mid-December to early January and included poetry competitions among others.

THE MARKET

The word market brings to mind an area with shops and commercial activity. However, ancient markets and especially the Agora, the market of Athens, was the first one ever made and was much more than that... Originally the Agora was an open area where merchants could sell their products on stalls they had set up. During the Classical Era, however, things were much different.

Silver tetradrachm with the glauka (owl), the sacred symbol of goddess Athena, 5th century BC

Agora – the ancient market

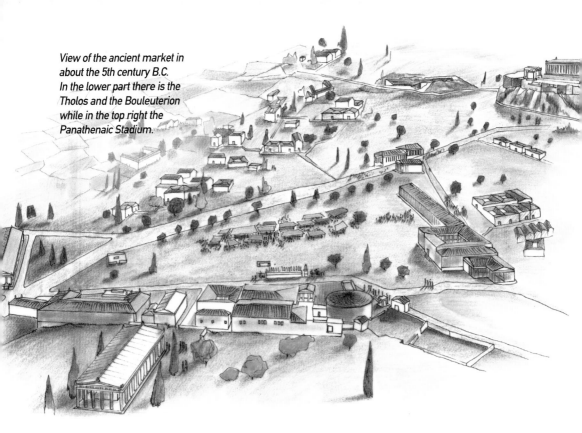

View of the ancient market in about the 5th century B.C. In the lower part there is the Tholos and the Bouleuterion while in the top right the Panathenaic Stadium.

In the late 5th century BC, the Agora started to become the center of political and public life in Athens. It is then that monumental buildings were built to meet all needs: the Stoa of Zeus Eleutherios and the Stoa of Baseilios (or Royal Stoa) which was the residence of the King Archon, as well as temples and altars dedicated to the gods. Buildings were constructed to house the function of the state government, such as the Bouleuterion which housed the Council of 500, the Strategeion, the Metroon where all valuable documents were kept and the Tholos which was the seat of the Prytaneis. There were daises from which orators spoke and springs for travelers to quench their thirst. Numerous statues, including those of the ten Heroes of Attica and the statues of the Tyrannicides (Harmodius and Aristogeiton) could also be seen. Finally, there were inscriptions with the state laws so that all citizens could see them.

The Agora of Athens was the most important part of social and political life in the city. The Panathenaic procession would cross it and all significant orators of antiquity spoke there. Over time, other large and important buildings were constructed as well, several buildings changed form or function, but the Agora remained always the center of the city and Athenian democracy ...

KERAMEIKOS

Originally, it was the potters' quarter of the city, while later the Kerameikos became the biggest cemetery of the city. There, archaeologists discovered tombs from several periods of ancient Greek history, within which very important objects, such as vases, jewelry, and weapons were found.

Funerary Monuments

At the current place of the Holy Trinity church there was the Dimosio Sima or Polyandreion, ie the tombs of important people in Athenian society. There Pericles is buried along with soldiers killed in the Persian wars. During the Classical Era, each grave featured stelai with a few words about the life of the buried. These complex structures were called houses because they look like little houses, inside which the reliefs of the deceased and other persons were placed. Some large marble vases were also found there.

THE BIG HARBOUR

The major port of Athens in ancient times, just like nowadays, is no other than Piraeus. The decision to make Piraeus the new port of the city was made in 493 BC by Themistocles. At that time Piraeus was divided into three consecutive ports: Zea, the Munychia (current Mikrolimano) and Cantharus, which is the current main port.

Piraeus was connected to Athens by the *Long Walls*, built between 461-455 BC. The traveller who wanted to enter the city had to pass through large monumental gates. The walls were a project of Themistocles supported by Pericles as well.

Their construction lasted 17 years and cost 6,000 talanta, ie 36,000,000 ancient drachmae! Such a fortification ensured that the Pireaus was the safest commercial and financial harbor of the era!

Themistocles

Zea and Munychia were military ports, while Cantharus a commercial one. In Zea archeologists found 196 neosoikoi ie shipsheds for keeping the ships – indeed the largest number ever found at an ancient military harbor!

Around Zea and Munychia several ship yards were also constructed. In Munychia, except from the buildings of the harbor there was also the temple of Artemis Munychia, the temple of Zeus, Asclepius Piraeus, the quarry and many other buildings.

Piraeus was inhabited mainly by merchants, sailors, resellers, rowers and captains. The city of Piraeus is the only one confirmed to be planned by the famous urban planner Hippodamus of Miletus. The city plan is characterized by order and regularity – principles of *Hippodamian planning system*. Actually, the market place of Piraeus was called the *Hippodamian Agora* in honor of the great urban planner.

The port of Piraeus was the center of trade: every day, numerous ships would sail in with all kinds of goods and sail out to their destinations with a new load. Ships were coming from the Aegean islands, the cities of Asia Minor, South Italy, North Africa, Crete and especially Egypt. Imports to Attica were of large quantities and great variety: silk, spices, precious metals, textiles, wine, oil, and most of all wheat. Five large stoes (galleries) were built around the port of Piraeus, one of which was *Emporion*, the commercial heart of the central harbor, Cantharus.

Representation of the shipsheds at Zea, Piraeus.

AND OUTSIDE ATHENS, WHAT?

THE SILVER MINES OF LAVRION

Lavrion is a town in southeastern part of Attica. In antiquity it was very famous for its silver mine, which functioned for 5,000 years and was one among the oldest ones in Greece.

The intensive exploitations of the mines started around 508, the birth of democracy and it was the main source of revenue of classical Athens. The first usage of the metal from Lavrion was to cut one of the first silver coins in the world, the Athenian drachma, around 580 BC.

In 482 BC a new vein strike expanded the gains from trade leading to another 130 trirems built. these ships helped the Athenian navy defeat the Persians at the Battle of Salamis, in 480 BC.

SOUNION

Cape Sounion is a promontory of Attica. It is the site of the ruins of the temple dedicated to the god

The legendary king of Athens, Aegeus, asking an oracle from Themis, who is seated on a tripod in the temple of Delphi. Red-figure kylix painted by Kodrus (440 BC), Berlin

of the sea, Poseidon. It was built between 444-440 BC on the ruins of the previous temple that had been destroyed by the Persians before its completion. Its order is Doric but unfortunately only some columns remain.

At Cape Sounion a festival was held every four years with warship competitions. According to the legend, this was the cape where King Aegeus of Athens fell into the deep sea upon seeing the black sails of his son's, Theseus, ship returning from Crete. He thought that Theseus had died in his attempt to kill the Minotaur. Thus, the sea where Aegeus drowned was called Aegean Sea – a name kept till nowadays...

ELEUSIS AND THE MYSTERIES

One day, goddess Demeter's daughter, Persephone, was picking flowers with her friends, when Hades, the god of the Underworld, who fell in love with her, seized her and took her to his underworld kingdom. Demeter began looking for her in every city, transformed into an old lady. Yet, no one would open his house for her... Only the King of Eleusis welcomed and hosted her. Then, she revealed herself and as a reward for his kindness, she taught him how to cultivate wheat... In honor of goddess Demeter, the Eleusinians introduced the celebration of the Great Mysteries and founded the sanctuary of Demeter and Persephone. The Greater Eleusinian Mysteries started on the 15th of month Boedromion and lasted nine days. After the processions, purifications and sacrifices in Athens, the sacred procession headed to Eleusis, along the Hiera Odos or Sacred Way. There, in the last night, the Hierophant, ie the one who shows the sacred ones, initiated the youths into the Mysteries and the worship of Demeter. But no one was allowed to reveal what exactly was happening in those rituals. The

Silver coin with the head of Persephone

only thing we know is that the rites aimed at the goddess offering fertility to nature. The worship of goddess Demeter and her daughter, Persephone was sacramental and both goddesses were patrons of the afterlife.

The most important building of the sanctuary, where the rites of initiation were held, was *Telesterion*. In the mid 5th century BC, Pericles wanted to build a new, larger Telesterion and commissioned it to Iktinos. Eventually, it was built by the architect Coroebus, who changed the original plans. As time passed by, many more changes were made in the sanctuary and several other buildings were built. However, votaries continued to visit it for centuries, to thank goddess Demeter who gave them wheat and protected them on their journey to the Underworld.

EPIDAURUS

Epidaurus was one of the largest ancient temples of antiquity. It was dedicated to the physician-god, Asclepeios.

Votaries would go to be cured from their illness at the Asklipieion of Epidaurus, and of course they had to follow specific procedures. They participated in the ritual procession, made sacrifices to the god, and then, clean as they were, went to the *enkoimeteria*, big sleeping halls where they spent the night. Asclepius would come in their sleep to heal them or give them advice on how to be healed.

The most important of the numerous buildings of the sanctuary were the temple of Asklepios, the Tholos, and the Avaton. The temple was of Doric order and its pediments depicted the fall of Troy and the Amazonomacy, ie the Battle with Amazons.

One of the most famous monuments of Epidaurus is the theater. It was built in the mid 4th century BC by architect Polykleitos the Younger. The theater is characterized by absolute symmetry. It is, probably, the most beautiful theater saved in excellent condition.

Asclepeion of Epidaurus became a model for many other Asclepieia, such as the one at Kos: it was built during the 4th century BC at the Sanctuary of Apollo. In the Asklipieion of Kos, which was the

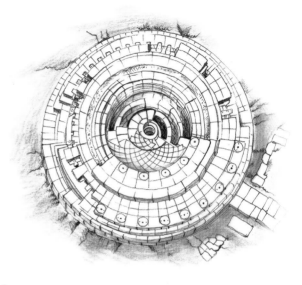

The Tholos of the Asklepeion of Epidaurus is allegedly the last circular peripteron (ie having single row of columns all around) building in the history of ancient Greek architecture

largest healing site of Ancient Greece, Hippocrates, the great physician of antiquity was taught Medicine.

DELPHI AND ORACLES

Delphi is located on the edge of a cliff, on an all-green slope of Mount Parnassus. The sanctuary of Delphi is dedicated to Apollo, who killed *Python*, the serpent which lived there. Then he founded his temple and oracle. From the name of the snake he had killed, the god also was called *Pythian*, while his priestess was called Pythia.

Apollo, a baby in his mother's arms, aiming at Python (draft plan from a black-figure lekythos of 470 BC)

Delphi was renowned for the Oracle as well as for the games held there in honor of Apollo, the *Pythian Games.* As Apollo was the patron god of music as well, music and mimic contests were also held there, apart from the sport events. The Pythian Games were held in late summer, in the third year after the Olympic Games and lasted five days. Pythian Games were under the *Delphic Ekechereia,* ie

Sports Events in Pythian Games

laurel

sacred truce, was compulsory for these games. This means that during the games all military conflicts were suspended. The city that would not respect Ekechereia was excluded from the games and had no right to ask the Oracle for a prediction.

The main building of the sanctuary was the temple of Apollo. The temple, which still remains, was inaugurated in 330 BC and is of Doric order. Its eastern pediment depicts god Apollo sitting on a tripod, among his mother, Leto, his sister, goddess Artemis and the Muses. Inside the temple there was the statue of Apollo and *antron,* ie the cave, where only Pythia the seer, could enter. There were all necessary items for vaticination: the ravine where vapors came out from, the tripod where Pythia was seated, the sacred laurel which was the

Representation, Delphi, Sanctuary of Apollo, Stoa of the Athenians

sacred plant of the god, the water of Cassotis Spring, the golden statue of Apollo and the tomb of Python. A certain process had to be followed for access to an oracle: the votaries and priests should be washed in the water of the sacred *Castalian Spring*, while those seeking a prediction would offer a barley pie and sacrifice an animal on the altar. Then, they would enter the adyton, Pythia listened to the question, drank water from the Cassotis Spring, chewed laurel leaves breathing vapors and coming in contact with the God. Then she burst into cries, gasps and yells, which the priests interpreted to the votaries as the Pythia did not come into contact with them.

Bronze figurine of a girl participating in sports competitions

All contemporary Greek cities and provinces participated, each with its own athletes. During the Games the Olympic Truce prevailed. Any city which did not respect the truce, could not participate in the Olympic Games. Only men could watch the games; women were strictly excluded. However, every four years between two consequtive Olympic Games the

OLYMPIA AND OLYMPIC GAMES

Olympia lies in Peloponnese, in a fertile valley at the juncture of the Alpheus and the Kladeus rivers. This all-beautiful place was the site where the Olympic Games, the biggest sporting event in until nowadays, was introduced in the 8th century BC.
According to myth, the hero Pelops was their founder who won the King Oenomaos in a chariot race. The Games were held every four years in the first 15 days of August and lasted five days.

The schedule of the Olympic Games
Day 1: athletes' swearing the oath and drawing for events
Day 2: young males events (running, wrestling, boxing and pankration)
Day 3: racing, chariot racing and the pentathlon (jump, discus, running, javelin, wrestling)
Day 4: males events: stade, diaulos (two-stade race), dolichus, wrestling, boxing, pankration, hoplitodromos
Day 5: nomination and award of olive wreaths to the winners.

Olympic events
oleaster – wild olive tree

East pediment of Olympia

Heraea Games would take place in honor of goddess Hera. In Heraea only maids participated.

In Olympia there were temples. The most important building was the Temple of Zeus. The temple was constructed by the architect Libon and was completed as early as 457 BC. It was of Doric order and was the largest temple in Peloponnese – about twenty meters high! Its pediments depict two scenes: the chariot race between Pelops and Oenomaus, and a scene from the Centauromachy. The metopes depict the 12 labors of Hercules, the favourite hero of ancient Greece. The temple housed the gold and ivory statue of Zeus, one of the seven wonders of antiquity. It was created by the sculptor Phidias and was 12.40 meters high! Zeus was represented seated on his throne, holding a Nike in his right hand and a scepter with the eagle, his symbol, in the left.

Elevation of the Temple of Zeus representing the gold and ivory statue of the god

Detail from a bronze coin depicting the gold and ivory statue of Zeus (Monetary Museum of Athens)

NEMEA

The temple of Nemea lies in a valley surrounded by mountains, near Corinth. One of the caves on these mountains was the home of the Nemean Lion – the one killed by Hercules in his well known feat. The Nemean sanctuary was dedicated to Zeus and was famous for the *Nemean Games*, the sport events held there both the year before and the year after the Ancient Olympic Games.

The largest and most important building in the sanctuary is the temple of Zeus. It was built in 330 BC and is probably the first building which combines all three architectural orders. In front of the temple there is the 41 meters long altar.

Near the sanctuary there is the stadium. The sanctuary and the stadium were connected by the sacred way, along which priests, athletes and votaries processed. Right outside the stadium there was the Apodyterion, the locker room. It is the first permanent building of this type, which survived. There, the athletes would leave their clothes before the games. Then, through a long corridor, they entered the stadium. Currently, this very corridor is still there just like in antiquity. There are still the athletes' names engraved on the walls by athletes themselves before the games. If you happen to find yourself at Nemea one month before the Olympics, do not miss the opportunity to participate in the modern Nemean Games! If you win, you will be wreathed in wild celery leaves, just like the athletes in ancient times.

Detail, Hercules kills the Nemea lion; Black-figure krater, National Archaeological Museum of Athens

65

CORINTH
AND ISTHMIA

Events of the Isthmian Games

pine

At the place where Central Greece is separated from the Peloponnese by the Isthmus, two important sanctuaries lay in antiquity: of Corinth and Isthmia. Corinth was a very important city-state, allegedly the wealthiest city in the ancient world. It grew during the rule of tyrant Periander. It was built below the rock of Acrocorinth and had two seaports, Lechaion and Kechrees. The most important monuments of ancient Corinth were its Doric temple, Agora with Bouleuterion, the Theatre, and the Asklepeion. Priene Spring, where according to legend Bellerofond found Pegasus drinking water, is at the Cotinthian Agora.

Close to the Isthmus was the sanctuary of Isthmia dedicated to the god Poseidon. Melicertes-Palaemon, a child which after his death became a deity of the sea and was buried in the sanctuary, was worshiped there. Another building of the area is the Doric temple of Poseidon and beside it the stadium. The theater was built in a natural nearby cavity. Over the years, the site of the stadium changed and several other buildings, such as the Roman baths, were constructed. Isthmia accommodated games in memory of Melicertes (p. 78), established in 582 BC by Kypselides, the tyrants of Corinth. Except the road race, horse races were also held in honor of Poseidon, the protector of horses. There were also rowing, recitation, painting, and music contests with a pine wreath as a prize.

Ino-Leukothea and Melicertes-Palaemon depicted in the sea, on a sea centaur. From embossed silver plate, 7th century BC, Benaki Museum

SPARTA

If you lived in the 5th century BC it would be a little difficult to visit Sparta... Spartans were brave and mighty warriors, but led a hard and simple life without any fun. They were not fond of the foreigners, thus they created the institution of *Xenelasia*, according to which no one could be accommodated in Sparta, unless licensed by the state. Sparta was an oligarchy and had its own state organization. For Spartans, law was above all. It was the only city that never changed its regime and was never conquered by anyone other than the Romans.

Kore pouring wine in a cantharus. Part of relief from Sparta, about 490 BC, Copenhagen.

Creator of the laws of Sparta, was the mythical legislator Lycurgus. His laws were called the *Great Rhetra* (Clause). According to the Lycourgean legal system, Sparta had two kings descending from Hercules. In time of war, one remained in the city and the other would go to the battle.

Sparta was famous for the hard training of adolescents, which started at the age of seven. In order to become good warriors, they performed daily many difficult physical exercises, learning, wrestling, eating a little – the famous black broth *Melas Zomos* – and wearing the same clothes all year round.

In ancient Sparta, money had no value. This was because luxury was prohibited by law and food was provided by the state in the form of syssitia. They used coins for specific purposes and for trade with other cities.

In Sparta religion was a rather important part of every day life, while out of the 50 registered temples of Sparta 34 were dedicated to goddesses. Goddess Athena was the most worshiped one, followed by Apollo. There were also many celebrations with games, dances and chants, just like in the rest of Greece.

BEYOND THE AEGEAN

So far several cities located in mainland Greece have been commented upon. In that era, however, there were many major cities located on the coast of Asia Minor which were also Greek. Some of them formed the **Ionic Dodekapolis** (i.e. twelve cities of Ionia): Miletus, Myus, Priene, Ephesus, Colophon, Lebedos, Teos, Clazomenae, Erythrai, Phocaea and the island cities of Chios and Samos. Center of the union was the Mycale peninsula. Each of these cities comprised some very important monuments and were renouned for their achievements.

Woman from Pergamon, 450 BC approximately (Berlin).

- In **Miletus** there was the significant oracle of Appolo, the Didymaion, at Didyma.
- In **Priene** there were the Asklepion, the temple of Athena, the Sanctuary of the Egyptian gods, as well as the temple of Demeter and Persephone.
- In **Ephesus** there was the temple of Artemis, which was one of the 7 Wonders of the Ancient World.
- In **Colophon** there was a sanctuary and oracle of Apollo.
- **Teos** was dedicated to Dionysus.
- **Clazomenae** were famous for the production of vases and sarcophagi.

- **Erythrai** was the hometown of the well known Sibyls of antiquity – women who could foretell the future. The Sibyls, when in extasy, would prophetize spontaneously, without being asked.
- **Phocaea** was one of the first cities to produce their own coinage.
- In **Samos** there was the Heraion – the great temple dedicated to goddess Hera.

Other major cities of Asia Minor were **Magnesia** situated upont the River Meander, where there was a temple of Athena, **Pergamon** with its famous library, **Kydonies** and **Aspendos**, with one of the best preserved ancient theatres.

FAMOUS ANCIENT GREEKS

THE SEVEN SAGES

All forms of science developed through the centuries first appeared in ancient Greece. According to ancient writers, the first ones to deal with science were the Seven Sages of Greece: Thales of Miletus, Pittacus of Mytilene, Bias of Priene, Cleobulus of Lindos, Solon of Athens, Periander of Corinth, and Chilon of Sparta.

Thales was born in Miletus of Asia Minor in 630 BC and died in about 543 BC. He was a physicist, mathematician, astronomer, engineer, meteorologist and philosopher. He was the first one who tried to explain scientifically various natural phenomena. He discovered electricity and magnetism, stipulated numerous geometric theorems, calculated the height of the Pyramids measuring their shadows, and predicted the date of the eclipse of the sun in 585 BC, one year earlier!

Pittacus was born in Mytilene in about 652 BC and was a politician and military leader of his hometown. He was renouned for his bravery in battle as well as his social and political wisdom. The people, in times of political turmoil, gave him absolute power to anticipate the problems arisen. When his office expired he resigned voluntarily. He died in about 570 BC.

Bias was born and lived in Priene of Ionia in the 6th century BC. He was well known for his sense of justice and his rhetorical abilities. He allegedly once used his own funds to free some women who had become slaves, educated, endowed, and sent then back to their parents in Messinia.

Cleobulus was born and lived in Rhodes in the 6th century BC. He was the tyrant of Lindos and on a trip to Egypt he is said to have restored the temple of Athena, allegedly built by Danaus. Also, he was a composer of songs and a poet.

Solon was born in Athens in about 639 BC and died around 559 BC. He was a major legislator, philosopher and lyric poet. He enacted laws to improve the life of the poor and indebted – most known the seisachtheia ("shaking off the burdens"), abolishing the regime under which in case the indebted could not repay the debt would become a slave to the lender. He gave more power to the people from the lower classes and strengthened the power of the courts.

Periander was born in Corinth in 668 BC and died in 584 BC. He was the tyrant of the city and according to the legend he was so cruel that he did not hesitate to have even his relatives killed. He was a social reformer; he legislated against luxury and found jobs for the poor while taxing the rich. During his rule, Corinth emerged as a sea power and thrived.

Chilon was born in Sparta in 600 BC and died in the city of Pisa in Sicily in 520 BC.

He was sober, virtuous, very intelligent and a major philosopher. He wrote lyrics while is alleged to have said "*to be Lacedaemonian is to love wisdom*".

Apart from the very important ancient Greeks we have already mentioned, it is time to know a few more famous personalities of that era. You see, many people who created history lived in ancient Greece...

Ictinus: a great architect of the 5th century BC. He was one of the architects of the Parthenon and perhaps the temple of Apollo Epicurius at Bassae.

Callicrates: a famous architect of the 5th century – one of the architects of the Parthenon. He also worked in the building of the Long Walls. The temple of Athena Nike on Acropolis is said to be his work as well.

Phidias: a great sculptor of antiquity who was born about 490 BC in Athens and died in 430 BC. His most important works are the enormous chryselephantine (ivory and gold-covered) statue of Zeus at Olympia, the chryselephantine statue of Athena Parthenos on the Parthenon and the colossal bronze statue of Athena also on the Acropolis.

Pericles was born in 495 BC and died in Athens in 429 BC of the great plague. He was a great politician of ancient Athens and served fourteen consecutive offices as a Strategos (General) of the city. The period he ruled was called the "Golden Age of Pericles".

Praxiteles: he lived in the 4th century BC and was the greatest of the Attic sculptors and one of the greatest ones in whole ancient Greece. His best-known work is the statue of Hermes, which is currently accommodated in the Archaeological Museum of Olympia.

Myron: a great sculptor of the period from about 480 to 440 BC. One of his most important works is Discobolus (the Discus-Thrower).

Polykleitos: an important sculptor of Argus who lived in the 5th century BC. He wrote a work on the principles of sculpture – the first of its kind – while his most important works are the Doryphoros (the Spear-Carrier) and Diadumenos ("Youth tying a headband") currently accommodated in the Archaeological Museum of Athens.

Cleisthenes: a great Athenian politician of the 6th century BC. He divided Athens into 10 demes (municipalities) and each demos into 10 tribes. Each tribe comprised people from all social and economic strata, thus promoting democracy. He passed all state power to the Ecclesia of Demos (people's assembly), thus establishing democracy; he introduced ostracism as well.

Archilochus: a lyric poet of the 7th century BC, from the island of Paros. He was the first to deal with the inner world of man. His poetry is rather about present than the heroic and legendary past.

Sappho: a lyric poet who was born in Lesbos in 630 BC and died in about 570 BC. She is known for her highly erotic poetry.

Pindar: a lyric poet who was born in a village outside Thebes in 522 BC and died in about 443 BC. He composed hymns for celebrities and Olympic winners.

Themistocles was born in 527 BC and died in Athens in 459 BC. He was a great politician and Strategos (General) of Athens and the main contributor to the Athenian victory at the Battle of Salamis. He was ostracized in 471 BC and committed suicide by drinking poison.

Miltiades was born in Athens in 540 BC and died in 489 BC. He was a great Strategos (General) and politician of ancient Athens and he led the Athenians to victory at the Battle of Marathon. In 489 BC he was accused of treason, tried and sentenced to death – but he was eventually fined to 50 talents. As he did not pay the fine, he was sent to prison where he died from gangrene shortly afterwards.

Lycurgus: a king and legislator of Sparta, who lived in about 800 BC. He established the political system of Sparta and his legislation is known as the Great Rhetra.

Draco: a legislator who lived in ancient Athens in the 7th century BC. His laws were rather strict and most offenses were punished by death. The expressions "draconian laws" and "draconian steps" were coined during his era.

Aeschylus: a dramatic poet born at Eleusis in 524 BC. He died in Gela, Sicily, in 456 BC. His most important works were the "Seven Against Thebes" and "Prometheus Bound". He won about 28 dramatic contests.

Euripides: He came from Attica. He was born in 485 BC and died in 406 BC. He was one of the most important dramatic poets of Attica. He wrote about 92 plays, some of the most important ones being the "Trojan Women", "Bacchae" and "Hercules Furens".

Sophocles was born in Athens in 496 BC and died in about 406 BC. He was a very important dramatic poet and wrote about 123 tragedies. Some of his most famous plays are the "Antigone", the "Oedipus at Colonus".

Cimon was born in Athens in 506 BC and died in about 450 BC. He was the son of Miltiades and a Strategos (General) of ancient Athens, continuously from the 476 BC up to 462 BC.

Euclid was born in Alexandria in 325 BC and died in about 265 BC. He is the father of Geometry and his theories are taught in the schools all over the world up to present.

Homer was born and lived in the 8th century BC in Ionia, Asia Minor. He is the greatest epic poet and left us two of the most important works of global history, *Iliad* and *Odyssey* – despite the fact that he was blind.

Democritus was born at Abdera in Thrace in 460 BC and died in about 370 BC. He was one of the greatest scientists and worked with almost all sciences. One of his most important theories was the Theory of Matter, while he was the first to speak of the smallest particles of matter in nature – the atoms. His theories are accepted until present.

Anaximenes: lived in the 6th century and came from Miletus. He was a philosopher and was preoccupied with cosmology – that is how the world was created. He believed that the origin of the world and of all things was Aether (air).

Anaximander was born in 610 BC and died in about 547 BC. He was a philosopher from Miletus. He was preoccupied with Cosmology, Astronomy and Meteorology. He constructed sundials and considered that the world is based on the cosmic

balance of the four elements of nature: air, water, fire and earth. For Anaximander the creation of the world came from the explosion of a fireball which created the celestial bodies.

Polygnotus: lived in the mid 5th century and came from the island of Thasos. He was a well known painter and his works were exhibited at the Propylaea of the Acropolis of Athens, the so-called Pinakotheke (Gallery) and the Lesche of the Knidians Delphi.

Aristophanes was born in 445 BC and died in Athens in about 386 BC. He was the greatest poet and satirist – considered the father of comedy. He wrote 46 comedies, but only 11 complete have survived. Some of his most important works is the "Lysistrata", "The Frogs", "The Birds" and "Plutus".

Heraclitus was born in Ephesus in 545 BC and died in about 485 BC. He was a great philosopher and believed that the unity of the world order is the result of conflicting and contrasting opposites. For Heraclitus, the material world was in constant motion and considered fire as the key element of creation.

Pythagoras: Pythagoras was from the island of Samos and was born between 580-572 BC. He is the founder of the science of mathematics and geometry. He stipulated of course the Pythagorean Theorem which is taught in all schools until nowadays. Pythagoras invented the pentagram, the gradations, the notes and everything else associated with music. His school and students spoke of odd and even numbers. This great scientist died of old age, at Metapontum of South Italy in 500-490 BC.

Archimedes was born in Syracuse of Sicily in 287 BC. He was one of the greatest physicists, mathematicians and engineers of antiquity. He wrote numerous books and discovered the lever and the principle of specific gravity of bodies, immersing them into water. For this discovery he exclaimed the famous "Eureka!" He invented machines for water irrigation, hydrolic clocks, lift pulleys and, of course, war machines. He was assassinated in 212 BC at his home, at Syracuse by a Roman soldier. Tradition has it that when the soldier entered his house to kill him, he stepped in the dust where Archimedes had been working. Archimedes said, "Don't disturb my circles", meaning "do not mess with my drawings".

Kypselides: the tyrants of ancient Corinth. Kypselos was the founder after whom the whole dynasty was named. Kypselos was born around 695 BC and died in 627 BC. His son Periander was his successor and one of the 7 Sages of ancient Greece (see page 70). The last member of this dynasty was Periander's son, Lykophron, who was self-exiled in Corfu after the murder of his mother by Periander. He never ruled Corinth.

Philip II of Macedonia: he was born in Pella in 382 BC. He was the son of the King of Macedonia Amyntas III and Euridice. He turned Macedonia into a powerful state and was the first to unite all Greek city-states under his rule. It was Philip's idea to campaign against the Persians and anticipate once and for all the risk of their expansion. His dream was fulfilled by his son – Alexander the Great, as Philip was assassinated by his bodyguard, Pausanias, in 336 BC, at Aeges.

Alexander the Great

Alexander III of Macedon, or **Alexander the Great:** he was born in 356 BC and was the son of Philip II and Olympias. Legend has it that he descended from Hercules and Achilles. He succeeded his father to the throne in 336 BC, at the age of 20. Almost immediately he continued his father's work and campaigned against the Persians; in 335 BC he conquered Asia Minor, Syria, Palestine, Egypt reaching the depths of the East. After Darius' death he was proclaimed King of the Greeks and Persians. The Persians welcomed Alexander the Great as he was not another tyrant, like Darius or their previous kings. Alexander protected the natives, maintaining and respecting their customs, language and traditions. He founded schools for the people of Persia and had his soldiers married to Persian princesses. In 327 BC he married Roxane, daughter of Oxyartes, a local Persian ruler. Roxanne gave birth to his son, Alexander IV. In the spring of 327 BC he campaigned against India, but he was injured in battle and forced to return. However, he had already managed to cross the Indus and Hydaspes River. In 323 BC, while in Babylon, he fell sick and died.

When asked to whom he would leave his empire, his last words were: *"Τῷ κρατίστῳ"*, that is to the best one. Alexander was the greatest general and leader of his era as well as one of the greatest ever in the history of mankind. He would reward honesty and loyalty and severely punish betrayal. He was always fighting on front line together with his soldiers. He lived in the same conditions and even once refused to drink water, because neither his men had any. He was fair to everyone regardless whether a Greek or a Persian.

Successors: the generals of Alexander the Great who claimed his empire. After his death, as Alexander did not name any heir to his empire, his generals quarreled on the succession. This conflict led to the partition of the empire and the establishment of seperate kingdoms. These were called Kingdoms of the Successors and were as follows:

i) the Antigonid Kingdom in Macedonia and Central Greece,

ii) the Attalid Kingdom in Pergamon,

iii) the Seleucid Kingdom in Asia Minor, Syria and Mesopotamia,

iv) the Ptolemaic Kingdom in Egypt..

INSTEAD OF AN EPILOGUE...

At present, one can meet ancient Greece for the first time in the school books and the more fortunate ones, on their Sunday stroll. We treat antiquity as a mythical, faraway age strange to us, when people made large buildings and magnificent statues; yet, without knowing why... The ancient Greeks, through their works, wanted to praise life, beauty, nature, gods and man. The potential in every human being... They left immortal monuments for their descendents to remember the past and learn from it. Not just as a rememberance of a glorious past, but rather as an example of what man can accomplish. Ancient Greece is a past which we should be proud of. It is a philosophical attitude to life. And all of us, regardless nationality and religion, learn that when we have the will, a lot can be achieved...

TIME LINE

CYCLADIC CULTURE
(3200 BC - 1100 BC)

BRONZE AGE
(2900 BC - around 1100 BC)

2900 BC: Development of Greek population and use of metals

2500 BC: Troy (Illium) is founded

1900 BC: Flourishing of Minoan civilization

1600 BC: Early Mycenaean civilization

1450 BC: Minoans are defeated by Mycenaeans. Flourishing of Mycenae

GEOMETRIC PERIOD
(1100 BC - around 800 BC)

1100 BC: Collapse of the Mycenaean Civilization

900 BC: Sparta is founded

ARCHAIC PERIOD
(800 BC - around 500 BC)

800 BC: Greek alphabet

776 BC: First Olympic Games

750 BC: Beginning of Colonization

612 BC: Draconian laws in Athens

594 BC: Solon's election and reformation of the Athenian political system

546 BC: Persian conquest of Ionian Greek city-states

508 BC: Cleisthenes opens the way to Republic in Athens

500-494 BC: Ionian Greek colonies revolt against Persia

490 BC: Battle of Marathon

480 BC: Battle of Thermopylae and Battle of Salamis

479 BC: Battle of Plataea. Greeks finally defeat Persians expelling them from Greece

CLASSICAL PERIOD
(500 BC - around 323 BC)

478 BC: Establishment of Delian League under Athenian leadership

461-455 BC: Construction of Long Walls

447 BC: Beginning of the Parthenon construction

445 BC: Conclusion of the Thirty Years Peace Treaty between Athens and Sparta

443 BC: Pericles is elected General

438 BC: Inauguration of the Parthenon

431 BC: Start of the Peloponnesian War between Athens and Sparta

430 BC: Plague in Athens

429 BC: Death of Pericles

421 BC: The Peace of Nicias: Athens and Sparta decide upon a 50years peace

413 BC: War breaks out again between Athens and Sparta

404 BC: End of Peloponnesian War and Athenian defeat. Sparta imposes to Athens the regime of the Thirty Tyrants

403 BC: Democracy is restored in Athens

395-387 BC: Corinthian War. Corinth allis with Athens, Argos and Thebes against Sparta

359 BC: Philip II is proclaimed King of Macedonia

340 BC: Alliance of all Greek cities against Philip

337 BC: Battle of Chaeronea: Philip wins and dominates Greece. End of city-states

337 BC: Establishment of the Corinthian League under Philip's leadership. All Greek city-states ally to fight against the Persians

336 BC: Death of Philip. His son, Alexander the Great succeeds him to the throne

333 BC: Battle of Issus

331 BC: Battle of Gaugamela

327 BC: Alexander conquers Persia and reaches India

323 BC: Death of Alexander the Great

HELLENISTIC PERIOD
(323 BC - around 30 BC)

323-281 BC: War between Alexander's Successors. Three successor kingdoms were established: Antigonus II in Macedonia, Seleucus in Asia Minor and Ptolemy in Egypt

215- 205 BC: First Macedonian War between Macedonians and Romans

202-197 BC: Second Macedonian War. Macedonians are defeated and the Romans conquest Greece

179-168 BC: Reign of Perseus, the last king of Macedon

171-168 BC: Third Macedonian War. Victory of the Romans

147-146 BC: Achaean War. The Greeks are defeated by the Romans who dominate Greece

31 BC: Antony and Cleopatra are defeated by Octavian Augustus at the Battle of Actium

30 BC: Egypt becomes a Roman province. Roman Republic ends and the Roman Empire begins

INDEX

GLOSSARY

Aristocracy: the regime in which power is exercised by a governing body or upper class usually made up of hereditary nobility.

Boxing or Pygmachia: a sport in which the athletes fight against each other with their fists. They tried to give as many blows as possible and at the same time avoid the opponent's blows. If the fight took long, the athletes had to ask for a "climax", where punches were exchanged and the defender could not protect himself. It was a rather violent and often fatal sport.

City-State: an independent entity consisting of a city and its surrounding territory. It is an autonomous administrative and religious center with its surface depending on its military and economic power.

Democracy: The basic principle of democracy is that power is exercised by the people itself. The governing bodies, leaders and authorities are elected by the people, who enact and votes the state laws.

Diaulos: belongs to the running races – a double-stadion race – in which the runners should cover the length of the stadium twice.

Dolichos: running race in which athletes had to cover 24 times the length of the stadium.

Hoplitodromos: a running race in which athletes covered the same distance as in diaulos, but instead of running in the nude, they were fully armed.

Horse racing: the race of riders on horseback. Since the athletes used neither saddle nor stirrups, they needed a good grip and balance not to fall off their horse during the race.

Melicertes: son of the king of Boeotia Athamas and Ino, daughter of Cadmus. Ino, punished by gods for her wickedness and arrogance, was pursued by Athamas. Terrified, she took her son and got drowned into the sea. The body of the dead child was washed at the Isthmus of Corinth, to be found by King Sisyphus. Melicertes changed into a marine deity, Palaemon. The Isthmian Games were instituted in his honour.

Oligarchy: the regime in which power rests with a small number of people, distinguished by royalty, wealth, family ties, education, corporate, or military control.

Pankration: the toughest sport. It was a combination of wrestling and boxing, with fingers used rather than fists.

Pentathlon: a sport in which athletes had to perform successively the events of stade, jumping, wrestling, discus and javelin throw.

Stade race: a sport in which athletes had to cover the length of the stadium once.

The Nine Muses: were the daughters of Zeus and Mnemosyne and the patron deities of science and the arts. They were the following: Erato of lyric and especially love poetry; Euterpe of lyric poetry and flute playing; Thalia of comedy and pastoral poetry; Calliope of epic poetry; Clio of history; Melpomene of tragic poetry;

Urania of astronomy; Polyhymnia of sacred poetry and hymns; Terpsichore of dance.

Thirty Tyrants: a 30-member pro-Spartan oligarchy imposed in Athens after its defeat in the Peloponnesian War in 404 BC. In 403 BC, after eight months of their rule, the regime was restored to democracy by the Athenians.

Tyrannicides: Harmodius and Aristogeiton, the two Athenians who killed Hipparchus, son of Peisistratus and contemporary tyrant of Athens, in 514 BC during the Panathenaic Festival. In their honor, Athenians had their statue made and placed at the Agora..

Tyranny: a regime in which power is excersiced by one man only without the consent of the majority of the people. In other words, the tyrant gets the power first then trying to get the people on his part to secure their cooperation.

Wrestling: it required both strength and flexibility with intelligence. There were two kinds of wrestling: in the first one, the wrestler had to throw down with his shoulders his opponent three times to win; while in the second, the struggle continued on the ground as well, until one of the two opponents concede defeat by raising his hand.

LITERATURE

- Buxton R., *Greek Myths – A Comprehensive Guide*, Patakis, Athens 2005
- Gruben G., *Sanctuaries and Temples of the Ancient Greeks*, Kardamitsas Pbl., Athens 2000
- Kerényi K., *Greek Mythology*, Estia, Athens 2013
- Liddell H.G. & Scott R., A *Greek-English Lexicon*, Clarendon Press, Oxford 1996
- Pekridou – Gorecki A., *Fashion in Ancient Greece*, Papadimas, Athens 2008
- Treuil R., Darque P., Poursat J., Touchais G., *The Civilizations of the Aegean Sea*, Kardamitsas, Athens 1996
- Walter-Karydi E., *The Greek House. The Rise of Noble Houses in Late Classical Times*, Archaeological Society at Athens 1996
- Valavanis, P., *Games and Sanctuaries in Ancient Greece*, Kapon, Athens 2004
- Valavanis, P., Palaiokrassa-Kopitsa L., Steinhauer G., *Ancient Athens and Attica: Historical Topography of Asty (the city) and Country*, Melissa, Athens 2010
- Domi, *History of Greece. Classical Greece*, Volume 3
- Domi, *History of Greece. Ancient Greek Culture and Art*, Volume 5
- Kazazis, I. N. Lyric poetry. *Archaic Lyricism as Music Education*, Volume A, Vanias, Thessaloniki 2000
- Kokkorou-Alevra G., *The Art of Ancient Greece. A Brief History (1050-1050 BC)*, Kardamitsas Pbl., Athens 2009
- Bouras Ch. T., *Lessons on History of Architecture*, Volume I, Symmetria Pbl., Athens 1999
- Orlandos A. & Travlos I., A Dictionary of Ancient Greek Architectural Terms, *The Archaeological Society at Athens*, Athens 1986
- Sfyroera S. N., *The Essential Greek Mythology*, Ellinika Grammata Pbl, Athens 2003
- *The Asklepieion of Epidaurus. The Seat of Healer-God of antiquity. Maintenance of the monuments*, (O.E.S.M.E.), Athens 1999